FROM GRIEF

TO *Joy*

A Journey Back
to Life & Living

D0273627

FROM GRIEF TO *Joy*

A Journey Back to Life & Living

enspiritus
publications

Omaha, NE

Donna Miesbach

ISBN: 978-0-9859318-1-0
LCCN: 2012944712

Disclaimer
A portion of chapters 1 and 27 were previously published in *Unity Magazine*.
Part or all of chapters 13, 14, and 15 were previously published in *Gleanings, A Bi-Monthly Discussion of Life Issues*.
Poems by the author that have been previously published:
Be Still, My Heart Is Like an Open Field, Traces of the Infinite, You'll Never Be Surprised, and The Mystery appeared in *Daily Word*.
We Must Be Mindful, The Key, Perhaps, and The Shore appeared in *Unity Magazine*.
Imprints was previously published in *Chicken Soup for the Teenage Soul II*.
Oh Centered Candle was published by Abingdon Press as a Choral Anthem. Used with permission.
Author's photo: Billings Photography.
The pictures on the cover were taken by the author in 1995 on Mount St. Helens 4 years after the third volcanic eruption.

Design and Production by Concierge Marketing Inc.

Printed in the United States of America
10 9 8 7 6 5 4 3 2

What Others Say about This Book and the Author

"An inspirational book about personal transformation and evolution."

Dr. Deepak Chopra

"Donna's story demonstrates how we can all transform the challenges that are thrown in our path into life-altering opportunities. Rather than succumbing to the inaction of sorrow, Donna's courage, determination, and achievements are an inspiration to us all. I feel privileged to be part of her journey."

Roger Gabriel
Meditation Guide

"Donna has done much research, much soul searching, and has learned to find beauty in all the things that have happened. Like so many of us, she has discovered that grief is circular, not linear. You need to go around with it more than once, but it becomes a widening circle each time you go through it. Donna has done this and, like the caterpillar, she came through her losses transformed. This book is a work of art and love. Highly recommended."

The Very Rev. Lea Marshall

"This is a heart-touching story of transformation that is both endearing and powerful!"

Jonathan Goldman
Founder of the International Sound
Healers Association and author of *Healing Sounds*

"Just when you think you know it all, you meet a Donna Miesbach and find out that starting over isn't all bad. She's given me new glasses to see the world through. She's given me new perspectives to look at almost every issue, and she's filled me up with a passion to start looking at things differently. I'm lucky to call her my friend."

David Humm
Former Nebraska Husker and Oakland Raider
Currently a color analyst on the Oakland Raiders radio network

"Donna changes people's lives for the better. I have the privilege of knowing Donna personally, and, at very special times, she gives me glimpses into her magnificent soul. These are precious times when she does this, as she teaches me much. By Donna writing this book, she has pulled back the curtain of her soul to many. Why she has chosen to share the most personal parts of her life with strangers, I believe, is due to her desire to love and heal others. That is part of who Donna is, and healing flows from her. To read this book is your gift from her, and a gift from above. You will get a piece of one of God's most beautiful women."

Greg "Coach Roz" Roeszler
Founder and Executive Director
Playmakers Mentoring Foundation

"Congratulations on finishing *From Grief to Joy*—what an accomplishment! I thoroughly enjoyed reading this manuscript and admit to being teary-eyed at the end. Your book is warm and inviting, and I felt honored as a reader to have been invited on such a fundamentally personal journey. I wish you much success!"

Tara Knapp
Adjunct English Professor
Creighton University

"With joy and happiness I fully recommend Donna Miesbach's book. She paints word art in your mind, which holds you in the presence of the story so that you are totally captivated. Her poems move me into a beautiful space that envelops me with deep spiritual meaning. She is truly a gifted writer and poet. I am honored to know her and to continue to receive her wisdom as I walk my path in this incredible lifetime."

Monica D. Traystman, PhD
Health and Wellness Coach
Meditation and Yoga Instructor

"This powerful, poetic work is an eloquent reminder that no matter how dark or confusing life becomes, the Light is always present. *From Grief to Joy* serves to lift us up when our journey may be too difficult to understand. Donna shows us how accepting the present helps us discover our gifts both to give and to put into action. Donna's book offers the skills and strategies that all ages need for this important phase of our growth. Donna's story is an inspiration and a blessing for us all."

Dr. Tommie R. Radd
Author and developer of The Grow with Guidance System

Contents

Poems by Donna Miesbach

To whom much is given,
much shall be expected.

Foreword by Dr. David Morehouse

In 1987, I was serving as a United States Army Ranger Company Commander, training Jordanian Rangers in their desert kingdom of Jordan. During a dangerous live fire exercise involving my unit and an attachment of Jordanian Rangers, I was struck in the head and knocked unconscious by a stray machine-gun bullet.

The experience ushered me violently into another world. It was here, in this altered state, that my life journey began anew. What I learned on that day about the world, and my connection to it, set into motion a series of events leading to a new identity, one juxtaposed to my present.

The months and years that followed were guided by information, often not solely mined from this world, which led to decisions drastically altering my life. In short, an eighteen-year military career ended, and a life of teaching began. Through this teaching I met my dear friend Donna Miesbach who over the years has inspired me with her manner and passion for life.

When life skips a beat or two, or changes direction without provocation, it can catch us off guard. These sudden shifts can prompt anger, bitterness, sadness, and regret, often making it nearly impossible to remember that our best is always under construction. However, it is simply life. It isn't right or wrong, black or white, positive or negative—it just is.

All of us have experienced to one degree or another some aspect of uncertainty in life. For example, we thought we would be with this person forever, and then we are not—life takes them. We aspire to become one thing, and we end up another—life leads us. We devotedly follow one path—life presents another. You think you are not ready—life says you are.

The key, and this is not a new concept, is to find the lesson in it all. In other words, each situation in life presents us with an opportunity to become an example or a warning to the world—be the example.

Donna has, through a spiritual intention, converted conflict into connection in her life. She is being the example, and this book is the lesson of her example. Her story is an elegant illustration of how to recognize that, despite how it may seem, the world around you is not coming apart; it is just the turbulence that is necessary to project you into the next level of life.

Death, failure, conflict, disease, all are conceptual illusions driving you away from the fact that one day the universe whispered a prayer and you were born. Do not be afraid of what this life brings you. Use it, and listen to those who have learned that in the realm of uncertainty—your destiny is found.

Donna walks this path. She has experienced it firsthand, and her message is a powerful communication inspired by practice. We recognize that conflict is an imperative in life; however, many of us allow ourselves to be crushed by grief, enveloped in self-pity and complaint. From the experience of others, we can find strength; we can summon the courage to press forward in life recognizing that anything is possible if we own our choices.

Conflict is life. There is no life without it; therefore, adapt, learn to turn the energy of conflict, trial, tribulation, challenges, or obstacles into a fierce compassion, guided by promise and possibility. This is Donna's message—honor it.

It is with great admiration and privilege that I write this Foreword to Donna's inspiring book. I know that many books will follow. I also know that a life of learning expressed in teaching and gaining wisdom cannot be bound between the pages of just one book, yet this work is beautifully done, complete and inspiring.

Upon finishing it, you will know more than you imagined possible about the power of life, faith, love, and compassion. You will find yourself inspired by this book of lessons. The life situation encountered is not unique; however, the voice of the messenger is fresh, pure, and true, inspired by the illumination of personal experience.

As you read, you will come to know Donna, and if you read with your heart, you will transform your present understanding of purpose, expanding it to new horizons, even reaching to the edge of knowledge and beyond. My friends, enjoy the journey inward this beautiful work delivers.

Dr. David Morehouse
President and Director, Remote Viewing Technologies, Inc.
Carlsbad, California
www.DavidMorehouse.com

Major David Morehouse, PhD, is a highly decorated former U.S. Special Operations Officer and Army Ranger Company Commander. During his term of service, Dr. Morehouse was recruited into the Central Intelligence Agency and the Defense Intelligence Agency where he was trained to be a member of the U.S. government's top-secret clan of psychic spies called Remote Viewers.

Considered by his superiors to be one of the finest Remote Viewers ever trained by the agency, he served as an operational Remote Viewer for three years. In 1996, Dr. Morehouse resigned his commission and became the premier trainer of the art and science of Remote Viewing. He has trained over twenty thousand students globally, and his book *Psychic Warrior* has been published in sixteen languages. His work is highly endorsed by Anthony Robbins, Don Miguel Ruiz, and Dr. Deepak Chopra.

Dr. Morehouse is the author of several books; among them are *Psychic Warrior: Inside the CIA's Stargate Program; Nonlethal Weapons: War without Death; and The Remote Viewing Book: A Guide to the CIA's Training Protocols.*

The Gift of Grace

Who has not longed for light upon the path or searched for meaning and purpose as life's events unfolded? Who has not wrestled with loss or separation and felt the pangs of grief? Who has not wished for a sense of identity but did not know how to pursue it, much less how to achieve it? Oh, yes, books abound on all these things, yet clear definitions remain as elusive as the pot of gold at the end of the rainbow.

So how does one find truth, or even approach so vague a goal? We read over and over of those who have entered its gates but feel no closer ourselves. To be sure, this is a tenuous journey, with no path clearly laid out for us, yet the fire of desire—of longing—burns steadily within us, calling us to a place we cannot fathom, a state of being we can only experience but never truly describe.

The good news is that we are not in this alone. Even while we may feel we are stumbling in the dark, the pull of that inner magnet is true and sure. It knows where we are going, even when we do not. This is why, even in our darkest moments, even in our most difficult challenges, we can rest in the certainty that we are being guided every step of the way.

Life's lessons are progressive, and they lead us to the deep spiritual communion for which we so deeply hunger. When we can understand this, when we can bow to it and accept the necessity for it, we assist rather than impede our progress, for one thing is absolutely certain—in God's economy, *nothing* is ever wasted. *All* things will be used for some good purpose.

If we do not grasp the lessons being presented to us now, those same lessons will come again in some other form. God does not give up on us! Our infinitely patient, infinitely compassionate Creator knows what we need and when we need it, whether we do or not.

Everything—absolutely everything—has led to this moment. It has brought you to where you are, and even now, you are building your tomorrows. You are moving ever closer to your heart's deepest desire. This does not necessarily mean your limiting thoughts and habits are gone forever. If there are any left, you can be sure they will surface again, but now—with your increased awareness, with your strong determination to stay the course, you will recognize them when you see them and turn them away, forever. You don't need your old ways of doing things anymore. They've served their purpose, they've taught their lesson, so bless them for the gift they contained and send them on their way. You can do this. We all can do this, if we will but try.

True, the path that leads to our deepest heart's desire is not easily come by, nor is it casually traveled when once it has been discovered, for it takes us into interior places where no one else can enter and confronts us with changes we dared not imagine.

Why is it, then, that we blindly pursue this path of our travail? Because we must! Because there is That within us that will not give us rest until we open ourselves to the higher plan. Doing so requires unflinching courage. It requires us to move forward with absolute trust and utter confidence that we will succeed, whatever the cost, for this is a voyage of the spirit. Even though the task may seem formidable, we are not in this alone, for we are part of that vast underpinning that gives us life and gives us breath and that, indeed, finds its expression through us.

Once this understanding is securely in place, we find we have much to lean upon. In fact, we have everything to lean upon, for That which sustains us is what brought us here in the first place. It is not just "your" path. It is not just "your" challenge, nor is it only "your" journey. It is a quest of the spirit, of That which lives and breathes through you. This is very good news, because That Which Is Within You is infinitely wise and infinitely strong.

The secret, of course, is in learning to trust this Guide in all that you do. Be aware of its presence. Depend on its steering, its guidance, for it is the Master Navigator whose all-seeing, all-knowing view can take you safely beyond the shoals of life, into the safe harbor of wisdom and understanding.

Then, regardless of what occurs, you are rooted and grounded in the knowledge—not the hope, mind you, but the knowledge—that life is working itself out according to the dictates of a higher plan. Even though you may never see that plan in its entirety, its all-sustaining presence provides both the comfort and the certainty that, on some level, all is as it should be, whether it seems to be or not.

Spiritual triumph, after all, must be won. It must come through effort and through diligent persistence. You must show your earnestness. You must prove your sincerity. When you do, you will find there is a part of you that will not—even cannot—be shaken. Therein is the gift of grace that attends all true seekers, that assuages the thirst and fortifies the soul in its endless quest for its source.

This, then, is a collection of musings by one such seeker. It is the story of where the path took me, willing or not, and the immeasurable gifts that even the most difficult challenges brought. I have no doubt there are others whose paths were far more difficult, just as for many the paths have been much smoother, but this was my path, and this is the story I have to tell.

As much as I would have denied it after my husband's sudden death, I know now that it really is possible to heal. It is possible to recover. It is possible to go on with your life in a positive, meaningful way. It may not seem like it at the time, but it is true. That is why I am telling my story, because if I can do it, you can, too.

And I hope you will.

ONE

When Time Stood Still

It was one of those beautiful summer days back in 1994 that you wish would last all year. But for me it was the beginning of the "long dark night of the soul." I just didn't know it yet.

I only knew when I got up that morning that something didn't feel right. I couldn't put my finger on it, but I was uneasy. No matter what I did, I couldn't shake that awful feeling. By afternoon, my stomach was queasy and my hands were trembling. Something definitely was wrong.

So many times in my life when someone has died, I had a sense of it before it happened. This time it was different. The feelings were all there. Why didn't I recognize them for what they were? Perhaps I wasn't "supposed" to. It was a question I would soon ponder over and over.

Just the day before, I had ordered an expensive piece of equipment for my music studio. When I woke up with such strong feelings of foreboding, I thought to myself, *Maybe I made a mistake. Maybe I wasn't supposed to do this*, so I called and cancelled the order. "Something is wrong," I told them, "and until I know what it is, I'm not going to buy this."

Later, when my husband, Neal, got home from the meeting he had been attending, I told him about the awful day I was having, how I was feeling so terribly insecure. He tried to comfort me as best he could, but it's hard to help someone when you don't know what's wrong. Desperately I needed him to hold me, so we stood there in the office and he held me in his arms. What I really wanted was to go into the living room and sit on the sofa, as we sometimes did, so he could hold me there. The first time he did that many years ago, it was so comforting that I fell asleep right there in his arms! He just sat there and held me until I woke up. We laughed about it many times.

It was sofa holding I needed now, too, but we both had a lot to do, and piano students were coming soon, so I didn't suggest it. I didn't think we should take the time, so we just stood there in the office and held each other close. I didn't know it at the time, but I had just given up my last chance for sofa holding, all for the sake of a teaching schedule.

Neal, on the other hand, was having a very good day. He'd been to an important meeting and had been asked to share his vision for the organization to which he had literally dedicated his professional life. He had always been "ahead of the pack," seeing how they could make a significant difference in the world if they just kept their sights high and strove with all their hearts to truly serve. That day he was filled with the satisfaction of having shared his dreams with those he had worked with for so long. I knew what this meant to him and shared his joy over his having the chance to speak his heart in such a special way.

When I came up from my afternoon lessons, dinner was ready. Neal and I shared the cooking, and since I was having a tough day, Neal offered to fix supper. It was a beautiful meal with all of our favorite foods. I could see how the pork chops with mushroom gravy, the potatoes, green beans, and salad had all been lovingly prepared. It was a special hour, spent going over the high points of his day, rejoicing in his good feelings, and ending with words of reassurance for me.

"These kids are so lucky to be studying with you! You make it *fun* for them. Look at their faces! Don't you see their excitement? Their anticipation? How they can hardly wait to come here? So *why* are you feeling this way?"

Little did I know, as I kissed him on the forehead before going downstairs to give one last lesson, that when I came up my beloved would be gone. And I have no doubt that when Neal went outside to check the sprinklers after supper that evening, he had no idea he would not be coming back. Life does have a way of surprising us when we least expect it.

It seemed so strange and still when I came upstairs an hour later. There was an eerie feeling in the air unlike anything I'd ever felt before. I looked around for Neal, but he wasn't in the house. I looked outside and he was nowhere to be seen. *He's probably visiting with one of the neighbors,* I thought to myself, and I went outside to see if I could find him.

We have an area of common ground in which our particular group of houses sits, but he wasn't there, so I decided to follow the street up around the hill to look for him there. It was deathly still. Why was it so quiet outside? Not even the birds were singing.

As I came around the bend in the hill I noticed a rescue squad, fire engine, and police car all at the end of the block. I wondered if the woman living there had had a problem. I knew she had not been well. Suddenly a woman ran out of the group that had gathered there yelling, "Won't someone please help us identify this man before they take him away?"

Fear grabbed my heart and I started running as fast as I could. *Oh, no! It couldn't be! Please God, don't let it be Neal!* But it was. There was my beloved, lying in the street. I fell to him and started talking to him, but he didn't answer.

The paramedics who had come so many other times when he was in crisis were there working with him, but there was no response. I wanted to go with Neal when they left for the hospital, but they told me to follow in the police car. Never in my life have I prayed like I did then. *Angels of mercy, please let him be all right. Angels of mercy, please let him be all right. Angels of mercy ...*

They did their best at the hospital, too, but there was nothing they could do to help him. Everyone on duty that night was grief stricken. There were so many times when we'd come close to losing Neal, but they were always able to pull him through. Now he was gone.

One of the paramedics put his arm around my shoulder. "I'm so sorry. We tried. We *really* tried."

I shook my head, unable to answer.

After everyone left the room, I just sat there holding Neal's hand, trying to absorb what had happened. It all seemed so unreal. Then, without even thinking about it, I began talking to him. All the things that were in my heart just came pouring out, and as they did, I sensed that he was answering me. It was as though we were intuiting each other, communicating in the only way we could. We talked about so many things. About the children. Our wonderful, blended family. How I would try to be there for them. How I would love them now for both of us.

As we talked, Neal tried to help me understand that there are things we still have to do together, and this is the only way we can do them—him where he is, and me where I am. It was a strange but comforting thought. It seemed to contain a seed of purpose within it. Later I would come back to that thought when I was struggling with my life, trying to make some sense out of all that had happened. *There is a purpose here*, I would tell myself. *I just don't know what it is.* Somehow that thought would get me through the day.

In looking back, I know what I was feeling all that day. "They" were gathering to greet him. They were coming to get him and take him home. It was not the first time this had happened. They had been there in the hospital room the time he ruptured an artery shortly after he'd had an angiogram. Suddenly the room was full of them. It was electric. I could feel their presence. I could almost see them standing there watching us as I stood beside him, holding his hand, talking to him. Medical personnel were rushing to put in more IV's, frantically applying pressure to try to stop the hemorrhaging, while his pulse kept going down and down.

"One hundred over sixty ... Eighty over forty ..." It was one of the nurses attending him. "Are you with me, Neal?"

"Yes, I'm here."

There must have been a dozen people in the room, all doing something different, all trying to help him. "Sixty over twenty ... Are you still with me, Neal?"

"Yes, I'm here."

"Forty over nothing ... Hang on, Neal."

"I'm hanging."

"Forty over nothing ... Are you with me, Neal?"

"Yes, I'm here." He looks at me. "You'd better call the church. You're going to need help."

"No, I'll be fine. I'm not going anywhere, and neither are you."

"It's still forty and no pulse," she calls out. They're putting in another IV, trying to keep something in his arteries. "Are you still with me, Neal?"

"Yes, I'm still here."

The doctors are saying they'd better take him to surgery to find out where the hemorrhage is. *No, there isn't time,* I'm thinking. *It has to happen here. It has to happen now.* The room is charged with the Presence. *Strength and energy,* I'm praying, trying to send him all I can, hoping that somehow he would receive it.

"Forty and still no pulse," she says again. "Are you with me, Neal?"

"Yes, I'm here."

I'm wondering how he can talk when he doesn't have any pulse. He looks at me. "You're going to need help."

"No, I have you. That's all I need. You just stay right here, and we'll be okay." He smiles.

Strength and energy, I pray, *strength and energy.* I could feel the Power in the room. It was so thick, it felt like you could cut it with a knife.

Finally, after what seemed like a very long time, "I've started getting a pulse ... I'm beginning to get a reading ..." Gradually the pulse returned. Gradually, the pressure rose.

How do you say "thank you" when your beloved is given back to you? Somehow, for reasons beyond our understanding, we were given a few more years. Precious years. Years in which we were able to have a group vacation with our children. Years in which we were able to take a special trip to Cape Cod to celebrate our twentieth anniversary.

Twenty years! That in itself was a miracle. From the beginning Neal had questioned the wisdom of our getting married. With his history of heart problems, he didn't know how much longer he might have. He was ten years older than I.

"It might not even be five years," he told me. I was willing to take the chance. Even if it was only two years—even *one* year, it would be more joy than either of us had ever known. As he thought about it, he knew it was true. It would have been asking too much of either one of us not to accept the amazing gift we had found in the love we had for each other. Now it had been over twenty years, and we had cherished every minute. We were incredibly happy.

There were so many times during those twenty-some years that we came close to losing him. If it wasn't one thing, it was another, but he had such courage. He faced it all and fought with all his might so he could be here for us, so we could have more time together, and I did all I could to help him. Our love was like a lifeline for both of us, and we did everything we could to sustain it. This time, though, there was no "discussing" it. The "decision" had been made, and there was nothing I could do to change it.

Someone told me once that the higher you climb, the farther you fall. I know that's true, but somehow it never occurred to me that would apply to the kind of joy we knew. It does. After all the hills and valleys we had struggled through, all the challenges we had faced together, all the triumphs and all the love we had shared, abruptly everything came to a screeching halt.

It was hard not having been there for him when he died. We had always faced these things together. Why wasn't I there this time? Somehow I felt I'd failed him. I was devastated. He was gone at age sixty-nine. There was nothing left. My sense of identity was shattered. My very purpose for being was gone, or so it seemed. Half of me was missing. Nothing seemed to have any meaning anymore. What was the point of it all?

I was wrong, of course. All was *not* lost, but it was too soon—much too soon—for me to know that. It would be almost two and a half years before I found out just how wrong I was.

Be Still

Be still, my soul,

and question not

The unseen hand

that wrought the plot

That brought you to

this time and place

For all your doubts

will not erase

The things that made you

what you are

And brought you to

this very hour,

So do not strain

or question why.

The stars are in their place –

and so am I!

TWO

Those First Early Days

*"Every moment of every day,
you are being led by a light you cannot see."*

To go from the heights of joy to the depths of sorrow was a considerable plunge, a plunge in which everything was turned upside down and balance was a distant memory. Survival itself became a struggle as I sought to make my way through this new and foreign land. Suddenly I was faced with having to find my way through a valley in which my every thought and emotion had been traumatized.

Recovery from such a shock was a tremendous challenge that required a great deal of hard work. I found myself wanting to focus more and more on my inner life, to search the deeper aspects of my being in the hope of finding a way to bring order out of the chaos that seemed to have overtaken my every waking moment.

So it was that my very suffering and pain became a lever that nudged me in the direction of spiritual growth. Thus my grief was the beginning of a reclaiming, if not a discovery, of spiritual strengths in which I soon found refuge. The challenge became a springboard to unexpected sources of wisdom that I might not have found had I not been forced to face these deeper issues and forge the courage to rise above them.

As I did this deep inner work, a new sense of identity emerged in which I discovered that, in spite of my loss, I was not less but more than I previously had thought. There is much to learn, and much to be gained from such a lesson, but in looking back I can't help wondering if there is a better way to deal with death. Must we wait until it happens to cope with it? Wouldn't it be better if we prepared ourselves—perhaps even educated ourselves—so we are better equipped to deal with death when it does come?

Because we fear death, we ignore it in the hope it will go away. Then when death does come, we are so shocked by its arrival that it rips us from our moorings and sets us adrift, lost and alone. It can take years to recover from the blow, only to have it happen again and again.

Perhaps we have played the part of the fool. Perhaps we would be better off to study death, to make its acquaintance, to try to understand it before it makes its visitation. Then, when death does come, perhaps we would be more able to meet it and accept it so the wound would not be so deep, the shock so great. A broader vision inevitably brings the capacity to see from a clearer, truer perspective, thus allowing us to see what the plan has been all along, had we only been willing to see it. That does seem a more sensible way to approach the problem.

If the unfamiliar and the unknown are at the root of our fear, then doesn't it makes sense to remove the cause of that fear? When we look beyond death, when we allow our gaze to travel beyond that vague border, wouldn't we begin to become familiar with that unknown territory? If it is known to us, might we begin to develop a level of comfort with it? Might our fear begin to lessen, our courage begin to increase? Might we even begin to enjoy a degree of wisdom—and perhaps even *peace*—we had not known before?

Wisdom is the harbinger of peace. In peace there is no fear. Only acceptance. And trust. That trust leads to a deep inner knowing that we are more than just this physical body. We are spirit, unbounded and free. We are here for a time, and then we move on. Yes, "we" leave the body, but "we" do not die. Knowing this frees us to live our lives fully and completely.

Of course, I didn't know that then, so coping with the present moment was challenge enough, and I had to begin before I could even catch my breath.

It was 12:30 at night. My twelve-year-old granddaughter, Courtney, and I had just gotten home from the hospital and were about to fall into bed when the phone rang. "Whoever could be calling at this hour!" I said, half to myself.

It was someone from the mortuary. The young man was brief and blunt. "We just brought in your husband's body. Do you want burial or cremation?" I couldn't believe my ears. His body wasn't even cold yet! Certainly I wasn't ready to think about that. Not yet. Not at midnight. Not ever.

It was a decision I would wrestle with for days. I didn't want either. I just wanted him back. Of course, that was just the beginning. So many decisions. So many things you don't want to think about. Somehow you get through. There must be some kind of emotional anesthesia that helps you get through those first difficult weeks.

I was grateful that Jean, our oldest daughter, offered to stay and help after the service was over before returning home. When she mentioned it, I thought it was nice of her, but what would we do? The question was soon answered. We worked from the time we got up until we fell in bed at night. With an active church insurance business to keep up, our own insurance policies to find, estate matters to deal with, and so on, there was no lack of things to do.

I don't know how I would have managed without Jean. My mind was in a fog. Suddenly, nothing on paper made any sense, but business matters of this kind were her forte. It got to the point where I would just hand her things, and she would label them and put them in the appropriate stack. When phoning was required, she did that, too. I just sat and watched, my brain too numb to process anything.

After Jean left, the enormity of the task began to sink in. There was still so much to do, and I didn't know where to find much of what I needed. Then, on one particularly trying day, someone from one of our churches called, needing some information from their policy. I always thought our office was well organized, but on that day I simply could not find it, no matter where I looked. Finally, in desperation, I just looked up and said, "Okay, I give up. Where is it?"

The next thing I knew, there it was in my hand. I was so amazed at how this had happened that all I could think of was to whisper a rather awed, "Thank you!" After a while, it became a sort of ritual. When I didn't know where something was, I would ask, and there it would be. Either it would show up in a place I would never have thought to look, or it would just appear somehow. I definitely was not in this alone. "Someone" was helping me.

That was just the beginning. More and more I began to sense that Neal was still with me. In fact, the further away I got from the initial trauma of his sudden death, the more I became aware of the astounding fact that it was just his body that was gone. The relationship was still there! The love was there. The support was there. It was as though the relationship we shared had expanded or resolved into this presence that now was so much a part of my awareness. I sensed that somehow, through Neal's death, we had become even more, as if to say that the love we shared was just the beginning.

The best *is* yet to come, and all that follows will be an expansion of our love, built on the foundation that was laid when we were here together. A purpose *was* being served, and in the end, it would be all right. Just knowing that made it possible for me to go on.

Even so, it didn't take long—two weeks exactly—for the weight of it all to come crushing down. The emotional floodgate opened. The dam burst, and the tears came. And came. And came. And they wouldn't stop. It started about four in the afternoon. At 9:30 that evening I called our minister, who was also our very good friend. "Lea, I can't do it!" I wailed into the phone. "I just can't do it!" I was ready to throw in the towel. This was far more than I could handle.

Lea understood. She knew this was coming and had been waiting for my call. "Oh yes, you can," she said. "You can, and you will." By this time it had been six hours, and I was still sobbing uncontrollably. It would be yet another hour before the emotional hemorrhage stopped. It was the first of many such episodes.

For me, this was just the beginning of what would prove to be an emotional roller coaster ride. I often wondered if these deep emotional swings were brought on by a change in body chemistry. That is what it felt like. It was almost as though a switch had been triggered, and I would literally feel myself going down. Then after a bit, the switch would click again, and I'd be on my way up. It was a strange phenomenon. The only thing I knew to do for it was to get out and walk and walk and walk in the hope that releasing endorphins would bring it under control.

After the first few times, I began to understand that these deep swings were just that. It helped to know I would come back up. All I had to do was hang on until it happened. Exercise was essential. Getting out and walking became a daily ritual. Whether I felt like I needed it or not, whether I wanted to or not, I did it. It was the only way I could deal with such great, sweeping emotions.

The fact that I was out of balance was obvious in other ways, too. I found myself doing strange things. For one thing, my speech was garbled. Things just came out backwards. I wondered if I would ever get to the point where I could talk sensibly. It got to be kind of a family joke, some of the things I would say. Or do! Like the time I watered the silk flowers until the plant died. Once I even put my shoes on the wrong feet! The last time I did that was when I was five years old. But I did it after Neal died. And the corker was when I wanted to make a phone call. I put my watch up to my ear to see if I had a dial tone! We couldn't help but laugh, and the laughter did help.

In fact, it was surprising the relief laughter brought. When I laughed, my brain seemed to function more clearly. The tone of my spirit didn't seem as dark, and I just generally felt a little better. Since there wasn't much to laugh about in those early days, I decided to seek it out. I started raiding our book shelves. Anything funny would do. I kept the material at the table where I ate my meals and started a mealtime habit of reading until I'd had a good laugh. It may have been a stop-gap measure, but help in any form was welcome.

Then shortly after Neal died, I received a letter from the Chairperson of the Board of Christian Outreach at our church. Neal was a member of this board and had attended their meeting the night before he died. The Chair thought I would want to know that Neal had asked the board to find a way to offer scholarships to children from disadvantaged areas to help further their education. While I was surprised to receive the letter, at some deep level I felt Neal was helping me decide how to use the memorial money that was coming in. The letter also told about a mentoring foundation here in Omaha and suggested they might know young people who could use this kind of help.

A call to the foundation soon produced resumes on young people in their program who would be graduating from high school the next summer. Reading their stories was heart rending. I was shocked to learn what these kids had had to do just to survive. We did give the scholarships the next spring, and while they were certainly appreciated, there was so much more these young people needed. Somehow, some way, I wished I could offer it. Of course, I didn't have a clue as to how I might do that, but the thought would not leave, so I did the only thing I knew to do. I simply asked, "How can I help?" and turned it over to the Universe. I felt certain that if this was something I should become involved in, the Universe would let me know in due time.

In the meantime, I was still searching for a way to get through each day while dealing with the myriad of details that one must work through in settling an estate. While the task was overwhelming at times, it was small compared to the questions that kept looming in my mind—What do I do now? Where do I go from here? And why? It takes a lot of deep breaths before the answers begin to surface. A lot of deep breaths and patience and hard work.

Not knowing what else to do, I resumed my work as a private music instructor and church organist. I just kept going. It was what I thought I was supposed to do. What I really needed was rest, but I doubt that it would have been possible to get enough rest to compensate for the exhaustion and emptiness I felt. It would take more than rest to heal this wound.

Something else that bothered me was the growing feeling that Neal knew his life was coming to an end. All that year he had asked me questions about how I would handle this or that when he was gone. He wanted to be sure I would know what to do, and he said so. He even went so far as to meet with his good friend Walt to discuss selling our agency once he was "ready to retire." Since Neal was feeling well, I didn't worry about why he was doing these things. In fact, we had talked about some of this before, but not as often as now.

As much as I appreciated our having had all these discussions, I deeply regretted that it never occurred to me to ask what was really on his mind. If he did sense this was coming, the fact that I didn't talk with him about it, or provide support and comfort to him, became the source of considerable despair for me. Surely he must have known, or why would he have made certain all these things were taken care of? I'd always tried to be there for him, as he had for me, but was I then?

In my blindness and deafness, was I absent in a way I should have been present? Why didn't I hear? Why didn't I see? What was he feeling if he knew, if he suspected, that time was drawing short? Loneliness? Uneasiness? Fear? Why didn't I ask? Was it because of my own fear, or just plain refusal to believe it could happen? Here he was facing his own mortality, and yet his every thought seemed to be of me, making sure I would be all right. How could I have been so ignorant? Did I really think I could prevent his death if I just worked hard enough?

Facing these issues was particularly difficult because we had always had the kind of relationship where we supported each other wholeheartedly. For example, several years earlier Neal had encouraged me to go back to college to work on a degree in pipe organ performance. It was a dream I had always held in my heart, and I was grateful to have the opportunity to pursue it.

However, with Neal's increasing health problems, I found myself cutting back on my class load so I could be of more help to him. Then one fall, we almost lost him three times within a week. We made it through that year all right, but the classes were consuming too much time. I both needed and wanted to be with Neal, to help him as much as I could, so I decided to take a leave of absence. The degree would have to wait. The university graciously agreed to put my scholarship on hold for a year. I will always be grateful I took that year off. It was the last year we had together.

Once I was no longer in school, we felt like children at play. It didn't matter what we were doing—working or playing—it was all fun. It truly was a gift. Then something happened that changed the complexion of everything.

Around mid-summer we learned that the administrator for the agency that was underwriting our church insurance policies had "misspent" a considerable amount of money, and now both the agency and the program were in jeopardy of going down. Neal was gravely concerned about the situation and wondered if he would have to move all our churches to another company.

When the fax went on in the middle of the night late September 1993, I didn't think anything about it. It had happened before. What I didn't know was that it was the beginning of the end. I think Neal must have known. He didn't sleep the rest of the night. Sure enough, when we got up in the morning the fax confirmed his worst fears. The church insurance program we were administering was in deep financial trouble at the national level. It was a nasty scene. We were going to have to act and act quickly.

With a January 1 deadline, how do you find an insurer, go through the underwriting process, meet with all your churches, give them time to make a decision, and get the policies issued all in the space of three and a half months? Let me tell you, it isn't easy. To say we worked around the clock to get it done could be stretching the truth, but not by much. It was literally four o'clock the afternoon of December 31 when the last church came in that was coming in. We were exhausted.

Unfortunately, it wasn't the exhaustion that concerned me. For years we had managed to stay one step ahead of the coronary artery problem that continually threatened Neal's very existence. Unable to process fats and sugars efficiently, his arteries periodically plugged up. Stress, particularly extreme stress such as this, was almost a certain promise of another episode.

We were grateful to have made it this far, thanks to two bypass surgeries, two angioplasties, and a diet and exercise regimen that he followed faithfully. The problem was, there wasn't anything left for the heart surgeons to work with. If they had to go in again, what would they do? I was extremely concerned about the quality of life he would be left with if he had to go through that again, so the episode with the church insurance program was like the tolling of the bell. Without wanting to, I could hear it coming, and I fought with all my being to try to ward it off.

We had always been there for each other, so pitching in was an automatic response. We dug in and did everything we could to beat the deadline. I kept assuring Neal that together we'd get the thing done, and we did, but the toll was greater than I knew.

Late the following May he went in for his regular checkup. His doctor had been trying a new medication in the hope of controlling the buildup in his arteries, so we were delighted when he called and told us the figures were great. "It looks like we're finally getting a handle on this!" I could hear the excitement in Hugh's voice. In addition to being a very fine physician, he was also our personal friend.

We were jubilant. "This could mean a few more years," Neal exclaimed, and we were hopeful that it would.

Two weeks later he was gone.

In looking back, it seems that life is a continual weaning process. We come into the world dependent on other people, but over the course of time we are forced more and more to rely not on others but on That which is within us that is both our Source and

Sustainer. It's about learning to put your hand in the only Hand that can lead you not only through life but through death as well. The learning process begins when death first enters our lives as children through the gradual loss of family and friends, and it does not end until we, too, face that portal which only the soul can enter.

How we deal with these losses, how we let our faith sustain us, how we allow that Hand to lead us, no matter what, not only determines how we approach that door, but also is integral to the teaching/learning process of which our example is a part.

It is said that children learn through watching. I think we all do. In seeing how others cope with the challenge that grief presents, we are forced to weigh our own beliefs and attitudes. We are challenged to search for our own inner truth as we continue to develop the premise on which we are forever trying to build our foundation.

There is considerable responsibility here when you stop and think about it. Accepting the inevitable and making peace with it enables you to find a way when there does not seem to be a way. It allows you to reach for the heights even while your spirit is at the depths of its grief. It makes it possible not only for you to go on, to find new meaning and purpose for your life, but to do so knowing that all is not lost, only changed. While that change can be soul-shattering, strength is forged from the crucible of our grief as we come to understand that this is not the end but rather the beginning—yes, the beginning of a new chapter in which we must pick up the pieces of what is left of our lives and go forward.

New meaning, new purpose, perhaps even new goals all contribute to the direction our life will take. Suddenly we find ourselves with a blank page to write on. What we put on that page is up to us.

I have believed for a long time that all things come bearing a gift. If there was a gift here, I was determined to find it. What that gift was would not become evident for what seemed like a very long time.

We Must Be Mindful

I think the angels
must have wondered
when they heard
that great explosion –
They did not know
that God was
making stars.

So with us –
when chaos seems apparent –
we must be mindful
that good is being formed
and even now is destined
to occur.

THREE

Coping

*"Spirit never stops sending its signal to you,
but you have to listen for its message in your heart."*

As weeks and then months went by, I thought a lot about Jacob and how he wrestled with the angel (Genesis 32:24–30). I was wrestling, too, and I never knew for sure who would win. Grief had its vice-grip on me, but I think it would be fair to say I had a vice-grip on it, too.

Much like Jacob, inwardly I had resolved that I would not let go of this until it had blessed me. I was determined to find the good in this situation. There had to be some good purpose or I just couldn't accept it. Tenaciously, I explored and dug and read and researched and probed my very depths and prayed and prayed and prayed. I absolutely refused to believe that this was the end of the story. It couldn't be. Somehow I would learn to fit the pieces together. There was meaning and purpose to all this. There simply had to be. All was not lost. There was an answer here somewhere, and I was determined to find it.

That was one side of the coin. The other side was that I was continually bothered by the fact that I was feeling sorry for myself. I couldn't shake the feeling that that's what grief is—feeling sorry for yourself—yet I just couldn't help myself. My sense of loss was so strong, I had to go along with it. I had been caught up in a strong, emotional current, and there was nothing to do but let it take me where it would. There was such a labyrinth of feelings, and I had to work through them all.

At times I truly wondered if there was any way out. The good news, of course, is that that is exactly what needed to happen. We have to work through all those feelings. If we do, we'll come out on the other side better and stronger than we were before, but I didn't know that then.

It's hard to make peace with death. It's such an unwelcome visitor. There were all those thoughts that hung around the perimeter of my mind. Why wasn't I allowed to be with Neal when he died? The things I would have done differently if I had only known this was coming. The things I would have liked to have said. The anger I felt over all the time I'd spent teaching when we could have been doing something together. Even though I taught out of a desire to lighten the financial load for him, now I resented the time it had consumed.

Such thoughts and feelings are only natural, I think. They're part of the process, but natural or not, they have to be faced. They have to be dealt with sooner or later. You can put it off, but you can't avoid it. The day does come when you must either make peace with it or be destroyed by it. It's a choice we all have to make, even though it may be a long time before we are even aware that the choice is there.

Eventually I realized that grieving itself is a choice. So is healing. While one can hardly avoid the initial trauma, or the intense amount of effort required to recover from such a shock, it is essential to recognize at some point in time that "grief" is a state of mind. We remain there by choice. We leave it by choice. True, we may not always realize we have such a choice, but the fact remains that we do. It is up to us to decide who is in control—us or the grief. Are we clinging to our grief, unable to let go of it yet, possibly even nursing it lest it leave us? This is not necessarily something to be critical of, but it does warrant our attention. If we can be open enough to look at this candidly, we can learn not only where we are in our recovery, but whether we have even committed to recovery as yet.

Clinging to the past does not solve anything. There must be a flaw in the perspective that makes it so hard to let go. We do not see this in nature. We can look all around us and see how readily nature accepts the fact of change. For some reason, humans are not as willing to do so. We want things to stay as they are, yet we know they cannot and do not, not even for a moment. Every moment is different from the one before, and will be different from the one that follows.

Nature gives itself freely to change, and out of that change a new landscape sometimes forms. I'll never forget my visit to Mount St. Helens the summer after Neal died. Everything was blown to smithereens when that volcano exploded, changing forever the landscape around it, yet out of that awesome specter, new growth abounded. The white, bare corpses of trees lay like match sticks on the hillside, while all around them, flowers bloomed. The devastation and beauty that walked hand in hand on those slopes spoke volumes to me, without ever saying a word. It was breathtaking.

It also caused me to wonder why death traumatizes us so. Death is a natural part of life. It's how we get from here to there. Life itself does not end. It only changes form. Life is precious, and certainly we should do all we can, not only to preserve it but to preserve a quality of life so it is worth the living. But isn't it possible that there could also be a quality to death as well? Isn't it possible that a peaceful acceptance might lead to a more peaceful passage as well as a healthier, less painful period of adjustment for those who are left behind?

I wish I'd thought of all these things a lot sooner, but as the saying goes, we learn what we need to know when we are ready to learn it. If such a lesson helps us meet our own death, as well as the death of others, in a more graceful fashion, then certainly much will have been gained, regardless of the suffering and heartache it took to reach that point in our understanding.

In God's economy, nothing is ever wasted. Because that is true, then even our grief can be used for some good purpose. If we truly believe that, eventually we begin to understand that there is indeed a purpose here. Finding that purpose can be a great adventure. We may even feel as though we are back in school, with great lessons to learn.

For me, the teacher had arrived. Its name was Grief, and the lessons came a step at a time. In fact, the steps were so small that at times I didn't even realize I was progressing. It was six months before I even thought about gratitude. I was down in Florida visiting my good friends, the Kelseys, when I read about giving thanks for what you still have. The message hit me right between the eyes. I hadn't even thought about that, but it gave me just the lift I needed.

Writing down what I was thankful for seemed to bring greater clarity. I realized I was truly grateful that if one of us had to go first, that it was Neal. I was also grateful that when the time came, he could go quickly. And of course I was also very thankful for all the years we had together. Then I began to think about how all that we were to each other was still enriching my life. It was part of the very fiber of my being, something I would always have. It was our gift to each other, and to this day, it still is. Yes, I was thankful. Very thankful. I just hadn't thought about it.

Even though the steps were small, my healing had begun. Perhaps it sounds strange to talk about being healed of such a wound. The possibility certainly had never entered my mind. Grief was something you lived with. We all knew that, and experience proved it. All my life I've watched people carry their grief around with them like a fifty-pound bag they weren't allowed to put down. It became their *modus operandi*, their way of being. "It doesn't get better, but it does get easier," I was told. Seeing is believing. I just expected my life to be like that, so when the time came, that is what I did, too.

Fortunately, you don't have to live your life that way. Life can get better. There is another way to honor those who have gone on before you. It was just too soon for me to know that nothing is ever really lost. Changed? Yes. But lost? No.

Not ever.

My Heart Is Like an Open Field

This is a growing time.

No way around it.

I must go through it

So why not embrace it?

Why not accept it

For the gift it brings?

'Tis there, you know,

In the secret recesses,

Peeking out from all

The dark and dusty corners.

Pain is but a sign of growth

So grow I will!

For this is the season

And my heart is like

An open field

Just waiting for the rain.

FOUR

A Place to Begin

*"It is often through our challenges and uncertainties
that we unearth the highest and best from within us."*

One of the things we promised ourselves was that Neal
would retire from lobbying after we got the church
insurance program back on its feet. He loved the political scene
and was highly respected both at the state and national levels. In
fact, he received many honors in both arenas, but now it was just
too difficult for him physically. The time had come to give it up,
and this was the year he was going to do it.

We planned to make a trip back East to visit family in the fall,
and then down to Florida to visit the Kelseys during the winter.
These were luxuries we had not enjoyed previously since he needed
to be at the State Capitol whenever the legislature was in session.
The trips were something we had looked forward to as a way of
celebrating some much-earned and much-needed leisure for both
of us. Difficult as it was to go without him, I decided to go ahead
and make those trips. I knew that was what Neal would expect me
to do, so I did.

Traveling without your mate, especially those first few times,
really brings home how different life is, how much you depended
on each other, how much you helped each other and enjoyed
each other. Everything you did was more fun because you did it

together, but all that had changed. While being together in your heart helps, it just isn't the same.

I happened to be in Florida the weekend of the Super Bowl, and my hosts had invited a few friends in to watch the game. Everyone was having such a good time. It was nice to be there with them, but over and over, as people laughed and joked, I wanted to cry out, "How can you be so happy when I'm in so much pain? Don't you know my heart is breaking? Why isn't yours?" At times my silent cries seemed so loud, I wondered why they didn't hear me.

I did try to enter into the festivities as much as I could, but a part of me felt dishonest about it. To laugh and be happy would be like putting a stamp of approval on Neal's absence, as though I were saying it was all right. It wasn't all right, and I felt that way with every part of my being.

Sitting there watching everyone have a good time was like a wake-up call for me. Why were they having so much fun when I was hurting so much? For them it was as though nothing had happened. Life was going on as usual, but then, how could they know? They hadn't suffered my loss. For them there was no pain. Finally it sank in that it was my thoughts and my feelings I was experiencing! What was happening inside me was making the difference! This was an important piece to the puzzle.

Feelings and emotions are the crucible out of which we mold and shape our life. I knew that. In fact, I'd known it for a long time, but when such huge emotions literally sweep you away, it's easy to forget that we do have a choice. Clearer than ever before, I could see how our feelings are literally the touchstone for all the events of life. It is through our feelings that we experience life. Those feelings are subject to our control, not the other way around. This is a critical issue, because until we recognize this, we are at the mercy of our feelings, instead of being in control of them.

In grief there is so much to work through that objectivity such as this doesn't come all at once. It may not even come for quite a while, but come it must if we are ever to break free of our grief and return to life and living. Just the fact that I even had a choice was a revelation to me. Certainly this was not a new concept.

Long ago, when raising my children, I learned that I had a choice in how I responded to life's events, but it never occurred to me that this same principle applies to grief. I always thought grief was something that "happened to you," something you couldn't control, but was it really? Perhaps I had been mistaken.

I began looking at my thoughts. Were they positive? What was their general tone? Was I choosing my thoughts, or simply reacting out of habit? These were important questions. Asking them meant I was beginning to take charge of my healing, and thus of my life. I was on the way up from despair. I was on the way out of my pain. True, there were still miles to go, but it was a start. Finally, I began to understand that while I couldn't change the circumstance of Neal's death, how I responded to that event was entirely up to me.

Readers may wish to try Meditation #3 on choosing your thoughts, which is available in the Meditations section at the back of this book.

It is hard to let go of the pain grief imposes. It's one of the ways we still feel connected to our loved ones. We cling to it out of a need to feel close, but clinging to the pain prevents us from entering into a new phase in our relationship. Clinging is a form of resistance that ties us to the past and prevents us from living fully in the present, but you cannot live in the past. It simply isn't possible. We try to by looking back, but that isn't where we are. Always we are in the present. As long as we cling to the pain, we cannot see what we still have—what we never lost. When we focus on the pain, pain is all we know. Releasing our hold on the pain frees us to enter into our relationship in a new and different way. It allows us to realize how very blessed we still are.

While this new perspective was important, I still wasn't ready to be happy. It isn't intended that we spend the rest of our lives crying and grieving, but there is a vast difference between knowing that and being comfortable with it. I knew that remaining in grief would ultimately destroy me, but how was I to get beyond it? The answers were there. I just hadn't found them yet. I knew Neal wanted me to be happy, but I had to want it, too. I had to be willing to go on with my life, and I still wasn't sure I wanted to.

Finally, I just decided to give myself permission to be happy. It was the only way I could get there. Once I tried to accept the change and make peace with the situation, it was easier to be happy and not feel guilty about it. True, it wasn't the same "happy" I knew before Neal died—it had a different quality to it—and while it wasn't the "happy" I grew into later in my healing, it was a start. It was a place to begin.

The Key

Ah, my child –
Mind is the key
For it is here
that you live,
It is here
that you accept or reject
your good,
It is here
that you initiate
change.
Whatever you would be,
You must be it first
in your mind.
Whatever you would achieve,
You must achieve it first
in your mind.
You see, my child –
Mind is, You are, I AM –
We are one being –
One Mind –
And all the rest
is but a
reflection.

FIVE

Cocooning

*"The higher our vision, the closer we
will come to Spirit's purpose for us."*

It's strange how the threads weave in and out of the tapestry of
our lives. Sometimes we see them, and sometimes we don't, but
they are there. They are *always* there. Time gives us the distance we
nccd to see the tapestry more clearly, to gain a better perspective.

It's hard to break loose from grief when you've totally invested
yourself in it, but I knew I needed to find a way to do that. I
needed a "fresh" approach, something that would help me break
out of my thinking patterns. Visualizing "what ifs" proved to be an
excellent answer. I began asking myself what it would be like to live
successfully with this situation. How would it look? What would I
be doing? What would I be feeling? How would I have changed?

Something else that helped was looking back to see how far I'd
come. When you're taking it a day at a time, you may feel as though
you aren't making any progress at all. Looking back gives you a
chance to see how you might be handling your grief differently
than you were before. It allows you to assess your inner strength, to
see what you're still struggling with, and to recognize the progress
you have made.

It was surprising what I learned when I did that. Not only did
looking back provide a new point of view, it helped me get a
clearer idea of how I would like things to be. As I weighed what

I envisioned against how things presently were, gradually the experiences that filled my days began to match the new pictures in my mind, bringing me closer to where I wanted my life to be. It got me on a positive track and acted as a catalyst that helped bring my life more in balance.

I could see that all the evaluating and sorting out, all the effort to make sense out of the upheaval, was forcing me to explore my potential. This meant letting go of the old and embracing new ways of doing things. It meant learning to stand on my own two feet. It was time to search for my completeness within myself!

During this time I began thinking of this period of my life as a cocooning time, wondering what new identity would eventually emerge. I began to understand firsthand what the word *amorphous* means. I thought a lot about the butterfly and all the myriad changes that occur to transform that worm into a magnificent creature with wings. How *does* the chrysalis know what to do to become a butterfly? There must be an innate intelligence there. Somewhere in its own soul, it knows what it must do to fulfill its destiny, to become what it was intended to be from the very beginning.

If this is true, then we, too, must have a similar intelligence in our soul that knows what we must do to become what we were intended to become at this stage in our life. I wondered how that process of metamorphosis applied to me. When I emerged from all this, how would I be different?

When the caterpillar goes into the cocoon, somehow all the things that composed its structure, however solid they might have seemed to be, dissolve, transmute, and transform into an altogether different creature with new parts totally unlike those it possessed before. New parts emerge that allow it to be even more beautiful, even more free than it was. New parts that allow it to fly, to raise itself above obstacles that once were so difficult to surmount. Even to float upon the breeze, to take advantage of an updraft that lifts it to new heights of being, new states of understanding, where the vision is higher and farther and clearer.

I marveled that such a remarkable transformation could occur and wondered if that, too, was what was happening to me as old concepts, once so firm and hard, began to soften. Boundaries that once seemed so fixed all but vanished as they became a thing of the past, as they changed more into a point of departure than a point of limitation. Thoughts such as these transported me to a new kind of thinking, which in turn engendered a new way of feeling. This, too, was a becoming, so that what I now found myself being was in many ways altogether different from what I had been before.

Transformation is a necessary part of life. Until we are willing to enter into the process with our whole heart, we cannot really let go of the past. We cannot let it be what it was—the catalyst that brought us to where we are now as we bring the new out of the old. Truly, our pain and our suffering, our heartache and our anguish, do mold and shape us in wonderful ways if we but allow them to expand our thinking and our horizons, for it is through these teachers that we become more. It is through these changes that we build upon the past and emerge with deeper insight, greater vision, and even a clearer sense of identity.

In some ways I think the caterpillar is wiser than we, for it knows when the time has come to build its cocoon, to enter into the process of change. We are not such willing creatures, by and large. Perhaps it is because the change is thrust upon us so suddenly. Yet, if we were to prepare ourselves, if we were to admit that someday this time will present itself to us, perhaps we would not fight the process so much. Perhaps the very act of accepting things for what they are would allow us, too, to enter into times of change in a more graceful way.

More and more I was realizing the importance of fortifying our souls ahead of time by thinking through—really thinking through—the deep issues of life so that when life's difficult moments do come, we will be better equipped to deal with them. If we have done our "homework," then perhaps such events would not be so traumatic.

In so many ways we are creators of our own trauma by how we react, by how we respond, by the thoughts and emotions we allow ourselves to entertain. Yes, there are choices to make, but then there are always choices to make. In the truest sense of the word, we create the quality of our life. We form our experiences through our very attitudes, thoughts, and feelings. Perhaps if we came from such a perspective as this, it would be easier to move into the cocooning stage when life has been turned upside down. By accepting what has occurred and allowing it to teach us what it will, we can indeed emerge victorious on the other side. Then we, too, will be like the butterfly, for our horizons will have expanded, and our depth of being will have grown immeasurably as we learn to take what life brings and call it friend.

Acceptance is certainly part of the answer. As long as we resist what has happened, we are stuck in it. It is only when we accept change and let go of the past that we are able to move on to the new. That's how it happens for the butterfly. It allows the change to happen. It surrenders to the process. So must we. Then all these elements will be free to mix together and create something new.

Grief, then, is the chrysalis in which our metamorphosis occurs. In due time we do become a new creature, reborn out of a greater understanding both of ourselves, of our purpose, and of our destiny. In the process, the innate wisdom that is always within us guides us through the labyrinth of life, allowing us to emerge, victorious and triumphant.

Challenge can indeed be our stepping stone, a means by which our destiny is embraced, our potential is explored, our victory is won.

Readers may wish to try Meditation #1 on acceptance, which is available in the Meditations section at the back of this book.

Perhaps

We are "earthbound" now
But what of then?
When the lesson's learned,
The bloom's grown full,
What is it then that I will be?
What turn within my destiny
Will come as I am born anew?
Something I've not thought of yet
But which awaits as, step on step,
 The thought is formed –
  The thrust is given –
   And there emerges
   Fresh and new
The thing that I've been growing to!

Perhaps the process never ends!
Perhaps each finish just begins
Another newer, grander phase
As God reveals in wondrous ways
The fullness of His Love!
Perhaps!

SIX

Emotional Transfusions

"Love is eternal."

Several months after Neal died, people began asking me if I'd seen him yet. While I had heard about people seeing their loved one after death, I couldn't help wondering if they were imagining it. My doubts came to an end when it began happening to me.

Strange as it may seem, from time to time the veil of separation lifted, and I was literally either with Neal or had a deep sense of his presence. While some might try to give a rational explanation to these experiences, such attempts cannot change their validity for the recipient. So powerful are these emotional transfusions that they move you in one fell swoop into another stage of your healing.

Looking back on it from where I am now, I am convinced that love bridges these invisible dimensions. The bonds of love simply are not broken. As I mentioned earlier, I had a deep sense that our relationship was still intact long after Neal was gone. Daily I could feel that we were still connected, that we were indeed still working together.

While working within the context of that relationship was comfortable for me, actually seeing Neal was another story. Those events were completely unexpected, and their impact literally picked me up and set me down in another place.

The first time this happened was on our anniversary. Neal had been gone for nine months. All that time his things had remained where he had left them. I needed to have them there, but now I was ready to do something with them. Much of his clothing could go to our children, so I set about sorting and deciding what to send. I loved to touch his clothing. I liked to hold his shirts and sweaters up to my face and feel his essence still in them.

Loving piece by loving piece, I placed them in their appropriate boxes, "talking" with him all the while. That done, I loaded the boxes into the car so I could take them down to the UPS. It had not occurred to me that the next day was our anniversary, but that very fact makes what happened even more incredible.

Early the next morning, Neal came to me. It's hard to describe, because I wasn't asleep and I wasn't awake. It was as though a "window" had opened and we were in another space. It was vivid and it was real, but it was a reality unlike any I'd experienced before.

We were ecstatic to be together again. We hugged each other, and held each other, and laughed and talked. Then I remembered I had just shipped his clothes, so I told him what I had done. Thinking he had come to stay, I said I had better call the children and ask them to send his things back.

It was at that moment I understood I had a choice. Somehow I knew he would come back if that was what I really wanted, if it was just too hard for me without him, but then I saw what that would mean. It was as though I was being allowed to look into the future both ways—with him and without him. When I saw what he would have to go through physically if he were to stay here, I understood how kind God had been not to require that of him just for my sake. I could not ask him to stay. I knew it was best for him to be where he was, and I gave my consent.

Even though it was hard to see him go, such a great sense of love remained that I knew we had done the right thing. For days afterward I felt an indescribable sense of peace. That visit played a large part in my healing. It was the first time I was able to accept Neal's death and be at peace with it. It was an important step forward.

I do not doubt that the thought of his coming back may sound strange. It certainly does not fit in with how we see things here. I can only say that where we were, wherever that was, it was possible, and it did not occur to either of us to question it. The possibility was just a normal part of our conversation, and the fact that we had this choice was accepted by both of us.

There were other times, too, when Neal would suddenly appear in my life. Six months later I was downstairs practicing on the organ when the phone rang. It was a woman in California who had written to me several years ago about a poem of mine that *Unity Magazine* had published. The poem had touched Marcia deeply, and I had responded to her letter.

The day she called me, she was in the process of moving to Arizona. The evening before she called, she had been sorting through a box when she came across my poem and letter that she had saved. Touched again by their contents, Marcia sat there and cried. That night she just couldn't sleep. For some reason she kept thinking about me. Then about 2 a.m. she started hearing a poem. It was so insistent that she got up and wrote it down in the hope that then she would be able to sleep.

The next morning she called me at 8 a.m. Even though the movers were all around her and noise was everywhere, she couldn't shake the feeling that she had to call me right then and share what she had written. She called it a "word poem" because each line began with a letter from my name. It was beautiful. She didn't know why she had to call. She just knew she would have no peace until she did, but I knew why. It was Neal's birthday.

We talked for quite a while, and when it was time to hang up, Marcia ended our conversation by saying, "Just keep on being the beautiful, sweet person you are. The world needs what you have to offer." I was deeply touched and felt that once again I had heard from Neal.

The following spring, Easter came on our anniversary, so the thought of new life and the promise of eternal life were very much in the front of my mind when I went to church that bright, sunny morning. I went early, as I wanted to be sure to hear the brass group that was going to play before the service. I could hardly believe my ears when they began their prelude with Grieg's *Ich Liebe Dich* (I Love Thee). Neal and I loved this song so much that we had it sung at our wedding. Over the years, we sang it together often as a duet. What was so amazing was that I have never heard this played as a prelude before any church service, let alone on Easter. I have spent a large part of my life in churches, and that had never happened before. They played all three verses, just the way we used to sing them, and there was no doubt in my mind that it was especially for me from Neal.

Two Distant Worlds

We live in two distant worlds,
you and I,
And yet we share a common bond
That all the differences
cannot divide,
And all the years
Or joys or tears
Have not the means
to separate
The love that makes us one.
Yes, we are not divisible
For we have built
a span
That long ago began
Within our hearts.

SEVEN

A Breath of Air

"Choose joy. Always choose joy."

There are so many "firsts" after a loss such as this. For a long time each one is almost like starting over. Visits to the children, traveling alone, hearing the choir sing without your loved one in it, going to the golf course alone, having *all* the errands to do yourself when you had always shared them. It just seems like it never ends. The newness does end, of course, but not for a while.

For me, the pain I experienced with all these firsts became my emotional barometer in that it indicated where I was in my lingering attachment to Neal. I certainly didn't realize how deeply entrenched I was in my widowhood. It had become my new identity, my only remaining "connection" to him, and I wasn't about to give it up. It was almost as though he'd gone on a trip and I was just keeping things together while he was gone. Of course, I knew he wasn't coming back, but that didn't change my attitude. As far as I was concerned, I was still his wife. Anyone who said otherwise was quickly corrected, which is exactly what I told the mortgage people when I wanted to change my loan from a flexible to a fixed rate of interest. After they changed the wording from "a single person" to "a widow," I agreed to sign the papers.

Time is a patient teacher, and the lessons come in many forms. Soon after my return from my trip to Florida, two good friends lost their husbands, too. My sense of what they were going through began to pull me out of myself. I understood their pain too well and wanted to reach out and ease their anguish, or at least try to. Over time, deeply touched by others who were also facing severe life challenges, I began to think less about myself and more about others whose paths seemed more difficult than mine. This concern developed into sort of an informal network, another step in the healing process that had come about in its own time.

Nor had I forgotten the question I'd prayerfully asked in what seemed like lifetimes ago, "How can I help these kids?" I did come up with ideas now and then. Sometimes they were triggered by what I saw other people doing, but I was never comfortable with them, so nothing materialized. Perhaps just getting back on my feet was enough for now.

Then one day in the fall, my good friend Marjorie called. "Quick! Turn on your TV! There's someone on the educational channel you need to hear!"

I did, and it was Dr. Deepak Chopra. I was mesmerized the minute I heard him. He spoke the language of spirituality I'd been looking for all my life. I took copious notes and studied them until I knew them by heart.

Two weeks later, Marjorie called again. "He's on again! Quick! Turn on your TV!" This time I taped the program and about wore the tape out listening to it afterward. During the program, he mentioned a book he'd written, so of course the next thing I knew I was at the book store looking for it.

The book turned out to be *Ageless Body, Timeless Mind.* I read it like a starving child who had just been given bread, but it left me with important questions. Deepak talked about honoring our body's signals, but how could I do that? And when he said our awareness changes our anatomy, just what did he mean? Then he talked about using a mantra when we meditate. What is a mantra, and how could I learn to meditate using one?

At the end of the book, there was a phone number with an invitation to call if I had any questions. Since I had three questions, I called. The person who answered was warm and welcoming. We talked for quite a while. When we were about to hang up, she asked if I'd like to be on their mailing list. I was getting so much junk mail that I hesitated, but this interested me, so I said, "Yes." I didn't realize it then, but I'd just found the light at the end of the tunnel.

The following January, a brochure outlining Deepak's upcoming courses came in the mail. Right in the middle was a beautiful picture of a young woman sitting cross-legged on the side of the mountain meditating. Beside it was information about Seduction of the Spirit, the course he'd be offering in Colorado that coming August. The brochure said we'd spend a week "looking deeply inward to find the source of all energy and creativity." We would be trained in Primordial Sound Meditation and receive our own personal mantra, as well as special sutras (unique mantras) for the energy centers in our body (called chakras).

The minute I read the course brochure I knew I had to go. I called and read the information to Marjorie. When she asked me questions I couldn't answer, I gave her their 800 number to call. Fifteen minutes later, she called me back. "You'll never guess what I just did!"

"Okay, what did you do?"

"I signed us up!"

"Well, then, I guess we're supposed to go!"

That summer was the two-year mark since Neal had died. I had come a long way in adjusting and felt I was doing a good job of coping. I had finished my interim organ job, I had two organ concerts coming up, and I had continued to teach.

However, in the midst of all this, an idea was beginning to surface. I had a growing desire to reach out to others in a more meaningful way, and I mentioned this to Marjorie. When she asked me what I would like to do, I told her I wasn't sure. Possibly through my writing. Perhaps through a newsletter where life issues we all face could be addressed. She jumped on the idea and strongly encouraged me to pursue it. She was familiar with my writing and said it definitely was something I should do.

That must have been all the encouragement I needed, because I decided to try it, if she would help. I knew I couldn't do it alone. I would need someone to talk with about it, to bounce around ideas with, to proof my work, to generate ideas, and more. She was delighted, and so we began.

Out of that conversation, *Gleanings, A Bi-Monthly Discussion of Life Issues*, was born. It brought new energy and zest into my life. I felt enthusiasm for the first time in two years. I was beginning to come into my own. It felt so right to me. For the first time I began to feel in "sync" with how things ought to be. It was like a breath of fresh air, and it really woke me up.

"Search for Identity" was the theme of our first issue. It was a natural choice. As long as I can remember, I have been on a spiritual quest. Even as a small child I remember thinking about the deep things of life, asking questions and wondering about life issues for which I still have not found answers. As I got older, I began to see life as a school. I still do. The process of finding what rings true in our deepest parts never seems to end.

Our search for identity creates a hunger within us that cannot be satisfied by material pursuits. Marriage, children, and fulfillment of long-held goals and dreams all contribute to a growing sense of who and what we are, but we seem to be caught in a circular dance that skirts our identity. We flit around it, but we never quite get there. Caught up in a ritual of outer pursuits and other commitments, we continue blindly on our way, but life has a way of waking us up—sometimes when we least expect it.

So it is that in our darkest moments, in our times of deep travail, we are finally able to disengage from our frantic pace and free ourselves from the clutches of all our busy-ness. Soul-weary and heart-sick, we have no other desire than to follow the inner pursuit, to fulfill the hunger we have felt for so long.

Crisis has a way of bringing our focus into stark relief. It gets our attention. It forces us to plumb our spiritual depths. It puts on the brakes and makes us look at what life is really about. Perhaps it is not this way for everyone, but that is how it has been for me. My "spiritual life" and my "working life" have always walked hand in hand. Even though there were times when one was more in the forefront than the other, they have always been like two sides of a coin, but this crisis changed everything. My spiritual hunger became the heavy end of the scale. It demanded my attention. It forced me to search my depths for what I needed.

Painful as it was, those times became immensely productive and fruitful. Thus, challenge became my friend. If ever I needed it, here was proof that all things do indeed come bearing a gift, if we will but look for it. The gift, then, was the growth I made, the inner blossoming that occurred as I worked my way through the pain and heartache into the sunlight that was patiently waiting for me on the other side.

Overcoming challenge is not a journey for the weak of heart. Even though we may feel we do not have the strength to face it, strength does come with each hesitant step we make. Gradually our spiritual sinews take on new vigor as we climb toward the summit of our challenge. Later, we may look back in amazement, wondering how we ever managed to come so far. It is then we begin to realize that ours has not been a solitary journey.

Preceded by untold others, we build on what they have left behind, even as we, too, leave some bit of light on the path for those who follow. Because we all are travelers upon this path, I longed to share the light I was given in the hope that it might ease the journey we each must make in our search for meaning and purpose. This, then, was what *Gleanings* was about. It was an exciting time, and we had great fun preparing the mailing, but when Marjorie left that day with our first issue in her hands, suddenly I was terrified. I began shaking and even felt a bit sick to my stomach. I tried to find her without success. I wanted to recall the mailing, but there was no changing it now. The deed was done and I was stuck with it.

Amazingly, my fears were soon allayed. The response was so warm. We truly had struck a chord with our readers. Perhaps we were on the right track after all.

Someone told me once to think twice before you start something, because you never know where it will lead. I didn't think about that when we began *Gleanings*, but the old adage proved to be true in all the best ways. Our readers began sending us their stories from around the country, and friendships began, sometimes in unusual ways.

For instance, there was the letter I received from Charles Doss. *Unity Magazine* was publishing poetry that both Charles and I had written. When he saw one of my poems, he wrote me, and thus began a friendship I cherish to this day. You see, Charles was in prison for a crime he swore he did not commit, yet prison bars could not contain him, for it was there that he discovered the boundlessness of his spirit. His joy was so great that poetry began streaming out, poetry that would rival Emerson or Thoreau.

Eventually someone offered to publish *I Shall Mingle*, a collection of his writing. His beautiful spirit touched me so much that I told my friend Marjorie about him. She just happened to have two copies of his book, and she gave me one of them.

To sit and read Charles's poems could only deepen and broaden one's reverence for the Hand that created us. What a privilege to be able to call Charles my friend! So of course I wrote about Charles, and with his permission I shared some of his poems with our readers.

Then one day another friend dropped in for a visit. During the course of our conversation, he told me about someone he knew who had been wrongly imprisoned and was having a hard time dealing with it. I gave him Charles's book. Even though it had become one of my treasured possessions, this just felt like the right thing to do.

About a year later, someone from England contacted me. She had read what I had written about Charles and already had his book, but wanted to know more about him. When she found out I had given his book away, she sent me another copy. From England!

I still hear from people who have come across his poems. Some of these people are also in prison and have found hope through his writing. Even though Charles passed on some time ago, his light still shines.

About a year after I connected with Charles, I came across an article in the local paper about David Humm. "Hummer," as he is often called, was one of the most outstanding quarterbacks in the early 1970s, setting records at the University of Nebraska–Lincoln that still have not been broken, but this article was about a challenge of a different sort. It was about how, even though Hummer's body has been compromised by multiple sclerosis, his spirit definitely has not. On any given day, regardless of how he is feeling or what he can or cannot do, Hummer will tell you, "Life is good!" and he lives it to the fullest.

Hummer's story touched my heart so much, I told our readers about him in our next issue. I also sent a copy to our local paper, asking them to please forward it to Mr. Humm to thank him for being such an inspiration to our readers.

Two weeks later, Hummer called. Was I surprised! I was even more surprised when we got to talking. We hit it off as though we were old friends, and thus began a friendship that has become part of the fabric of our lives. The more I learned about Hummer, the more intrigued I became by his story, so one day, after he shared a particularly poignant incident with me, I sat down and wrote the article, "… But Life Is Good," and sent it to Hummer. He was delighted and started sending it to anyone he thought would like to read it. [You can read the article at www.DonnaMiesbach.com. Click on the Gleanings page. The article is in the archives.]

As the years went by, I've gotten to watch his daughter, Courtney, grow up and go to college, and he has "been there" for me and shared in all the things that were happening in my life, too—and all because of our little publication!

Publishing *Gleanings* was a special joy for me. Writing was something I had always enjoyed. From my very earliest years in school, being an author was a dream I had cherished deep inside me. I didn't know why. I just wanted to write. Even as early as second grade, I remember walking to school, pencil and paper in hand, the "world-famous author" writing her first book, a book all the world was waiting to read. With all that "deep thinking," many times it was all I could do to get to school on time. Not that much ever ended up on the page. You would think, with all that preoccupation, that great streams of words would have fallen on the paper, but rarely did anything get written down. Probably because I didn't have anything to say—yet.

Before long, poetry was added to my passion. I loved reading it and spent hours lost in its magic. I even tried writing it, but it never really worked for me during those early years. It always came out contrived, stiff, and awkward. The desire was there, but the time had not yet come for the seed to blossom. It wasn't until many years later that it happened, and when it did, it began of its own accord.

We had been at a convention in Florida. The ocean has always been a special place—even a spiritual place—for me, so I spent a lot of time just sitting on the shore, digging for shells and listening to the roll of the waves, silently soaking in the timelessness I feel when I'm near the ocean. Being there always seems to feed me, and I'd been feeding all week.

On the morning of the day we were to leave for home, I was down at the beach one last time when it happened. That's when the channel opened up and the words to the poem, The Shore, came pouring out as the synthesis of all the years, and all the joys and sorrows, all the inner study and soul searching, all the everything came together in that one poem. It spoke reams to me, and even today when I read it, there is something new in it for me. I had it down on paper before we ever left for the airport, and all the way home I marveled at this wonderful jewel that had dropped in my lap. It was truly amazing, and to me it still is.

That was just the beginning. From that time forward I would see many poems in print, many articles published, and now here I was, trying to do a publication of my own. It was scary, but the words just seemed to flow. It felt right. I was getting "help," and I knew it. You can't do that kind of thing alone—and I wasn't!

Gradually our little publication grew and grew, until finally we decided to offer it for subscription. The response of our readers was heartwarming. More and more I began to have a sense that this was part of the gift that all things come bearing, that it was part of the "something we need to do together," and this was the only way it could happen. Could it be? Was it possible that out of a heart's desire to reach out to others, I might find a purpose, even a meaning to all this? I could only watch and wait and see.

The Shore

I stand on the edge of consciousness
where I am not so much myself
as I just simply Am.
In this moment of peace
I enter into the sea of Pure Being
and am caught up in the
wonder of this spirit,
so fluid,
so alive,
yet so still and so silent that the
sheer force of it fills me with
feelings that have no words, and
thoughts that have not yet found their
meanings in the depths of my mortal mind,

And yet, in their own
symphony of soundless sound, the
meanings are clear, and the
sounds ring through me with a
clarity and trueness that tells me
that This is the Truth of all Being,
the symphony of my soul,
the harmony of life –
and that even as I return to the
shore of my own personal self, the
Truth I have felt and heard will remain
as an indelible part of my being, and
the songs I will sing will flow out from
these depths where time and again
I will return
to fill the cup,
to refresh and renew the soul,
to be One in that infinite moment
where, alone with my Creator and my God,
all is answered
and all is complete
and there is only
One.

EIGHT

The Identity Issue

"The inescapable promise has always been within us."

As any good warrior will tell you, victories are won courageous step by courageous step. This applies to grief as well.

Sometimes we don't even know we are "winning." We may feel as though we are going backward when actually the very act of facing our issues and grappling with them enables us to go forward. That is exactly where I found myself by the time the second summer after Neal's death came. I was utterly and totally depleted. Even though I had finished my lengthy position as interim church organist, my large teaching load and the two organ concerts were just too much. I had driven myself to the limit fulfilling responsibilities and commitments I had made, and my body was screaming at me. I had no choice but to stop and listen. It was that or collapse, and I knew it.

Many times those who are grieving fall into this "busy" mode simply because they do not know what else to do. Busy yourself with all manner of things and perhaps the pain will not find you. Fill your days with meaningless accomplishment and fool yourself into believing you have a full and productive life, but it is all ashes, for meaning and value can only be found within us. To neglect our inner needs for the sake of "accomplishment" is to feed the ego and starve the soul.

Unfortunately, this kind of busy-ness has become a way of life in our culture. We spend our lives doing, doing, doing, while the inner self goes unfed and unattended. In the process, we lose sight of all that truly feeds us and gives our life depth and meaning. How much better it would be if we could find our inner domain and live from that perspective. Then what we do would reflect so much more clearly what we are. In that act of be-ing, our deepest desires would be fulfilled. Until we connect with our inner identity, it will be as though we are living with a stranger, someone we have never met whose name we do not even know.

I doubt that I will ever forget the sudden realization that hit me the night Neal died. As I stood there beside his lifeless form, I saw how all the things we had been trying so hard to accomplish weren't important. Not really important. Not in the larger sweep of things. We had been driving ourselves over nothing. Absolutely nothing. Oh yes, they seemed important at the time, and perhaps they were, in a way. But in the context of the picture I was now facing, they weren't important at all. In that moment, they were as ashes in my mouth.

I saw, too, how our whole lives seem to be wrapped around accumulating things. I remember too well how I used to think that if I just had this, or just had that, then I would be happy. Well, I was wrong. "Things" can't bring happiness, not the kind of happiness that truly satisfies. "Things" never really satisfy. "Things" change. They burden us with responsibility and keep us busy taking care of them, but they do not feed us. They do not nourish the innermost part of our being. Instead, they build a maze around us in which we become more and more entangled and lost.

We have forgotten that the happiness we hunger for has to come from within. The real treasures are things you can't buy— the touch of a hand, a smile, a kindness, memories that warm the heart and last forever, and, of course, the peace you can only find in your soul. Once you truly know that and base your life from that perspective, then it is easier to enter into all the daily routines without becoming trapped. When your happiness isn't dependent on what's outside you, your happiness is secure, and you are at peace.

When there is peace in the soul, how can there be fear? When we are caught up in joy, how can there be sorrow? And if we are at home with our boundless, eternal nature, how then will we view death?

It must have been this kind of thinking that had been at the front of my mind the day I was listening to my granddaughter talk about her wedding plans, hearing her excitement over the gifts they were receiving, the things they were going to buy, all the "stuff" they wanted to have. I remember having felt that way. It's a happy feeling, a wonderful feeling, but all I could say to her on that particular day was, "That's all very nice, but in the end, you know, it's only ashes." That must have seemed like a strange thing for me to say, but it was true. In the end, it all is only ashes. Real happiness never comes with a price tag.

Never.

Unfortunately, many times focusing on our inner life is a choice we do not even know we have, so we squander the gift of each day by filling it with meaningless pursuits, giving no thought to where we came from, or where we will be going when we leave here. This lifetime is but the blink of an eye in the scale of eternity— precious by its very brevity. We come, and we go, like butterflies in the summer, never reckoning that this day is the only day we will have here. This moment is the only moment we will know. How dear a commodity it is! It is as though all of eternity has been compressed into this instant. Its beauty and magnificence and incomprehensible scope—all a gift to us ... here ... now. And what do we do? We poke around in the ashes, hoping to leave a mark that will not blow away in the wind.

I do not deny it. I've been as guilty of this as anyone. I lived my life on "automatic" for much too long. Now it was time to be the physician of my own soul. It was time to stop and listen to my body. It was time to nurture myself. Both my body and my soul needed a lot of tending to bring them back into balance. Rest.

Good food. Replenishment. It had been too long since I paid attention to my inner needs.

When a person is that depleted, how do you bring balance back into your life? Emotionally, physically, and just about any other way, things are out of whack. It's almost like trying to put a broken dish back together. Where do you begin? A piece here. A piece there. Gradually it begins to come together. True, life will never be quite the same, but sometimes what does emerge is even better than what was there before. Perhaps "better" isn't the right word. Perhaps "richer" is more apt. I say "richer" because that is what happens when you allow change to be your teacher. When you allow it to spur you on to new growth. When you let it guide you as you build a new foundation for your life.

Pain—physical or otherwise—is our system's way of reminding us that something is missing. Joy and wholeness are still there inside us. We just have to be willing to go deep enough to find them.

I began by trying to answer the most immediate needs first. For me that meant listening to my body and then doing what my system wanted so my body could start functioning better. To help me do that I began reading everything I could find about nutrition and exercise and natural methods of restoring balance in the body. It helped a lot. It wasn't the whole answer, but it was part of the answer. It was a piece to the puzzle.

Just as important was the need to just stop and be for a while. I hadn't yet given myself the chance to do that, and I knew I would never be truly whole again until I did, so I took the summer off. It was one of the smartest things I've ever done. No teaching. No organ jobs. Just relaxing, resting, reading, playing golf, seeing friends and family, and a lot of "porch time" where I could sit and think.

And of course, there was the writing. That was a special joy. Not only was it deeply satisfying to be able to share my thoughts with others, writing also proved to be an invaluable way for me to process the events of the past two years, to sort out my thoughts and feelings and make some comprehensible sense out of them.

My body thanked me in a lot of ways. I began to eat better, feel better, rest better. More importantly, I began to feel less fragmented. Finally, I had the time I needed to think about what was really important to me, where I was in my life, and where I should go from here. We don't think about these things—not really think about them—when our days are full to the brim. It takes quiet time, time for reflection, time for *not* doing before thoughts like that will surface. It was a good feeling. Something was happening on the inside, even if I didn't fully understand what it was.

Being "too busy" is a problem that is not exclusive to those who are grieving. I've wondered for a long time if the reason we push ourselves so hard in our work is because we feel so lost. We try this for a while, and then we do that for a while, but always we are searching. We are trying to find ourselves, but we're looking in the wrong place. We would do well to stop and ask ourselves who we are when we are not doing these things. Who are we then?

Unfortunately, for many of us our true identity gets lost in our pursuit of outer achievements, but without a knowledge of who we really are, all the success in the world will not satisfy us. As long as we build our lives around outer activity, the hunger will still be inside us. It isn't so much a case of misplaced values as it is of misplaced identity. We just don't *know* Who We Are.

That was certainly part of the problem for me. My sense of wholeness was so wrapped up in what I was for Neal that I forgot what I was for myself. That's all right, because what we had together was far more than I'd ever had before. The wholeness I found with Neal allowed a lot of healing to occur, healing that was necessary if I was ever going to be able to grow into myself.

The only problem is, when you are dependent on someone else for your identity, once the other person is gone, what do you have left? Not only have you lost your beloved, your sense of identity is deeply shaken. I didn't realize it at the time, of course, but that was exactly what had to happen before it would ever occur to me to take the next step. As long as Neal was here, I was content to see my wholeness through him, but now I couldn't lean on him.

It was time to plumb my own inner resources. It was time to be me—simply and uniquely me. That would please Neal. He would like it that I was ready to do that. He always knew I could. Now it was time to begin.

Exploring our own inner nature opens amazing doors, doors that allow us to discover what we are capable of being, of doing—indeed, of what we already are but have forgotten. Until we find our inner core, we will always be searching. It is our sense of separation from that core that causes us to feel so empty. That is why exploring our inner domain is such a great adventure, and it never ends.

It took me a while to figure that out, but when I did, that realization lifted me right out of dead center and back into the everyday business of living my life, instead of just getting through it. Reading became a passion. Everything I read acted as my own personal sounding board as I listened inwardly to see what rang true.

The more I read, the more one thought kept surfacing, and that was that we are already whole! When things get out of balance, we just need to restore our memory of wholeness. I'd heard that many times, but this was the first time I felt that way. The more I thought about it, the more I sensed that wholeness really is an innate part of our nature, so I set about seeking to re-claim and re-discover the part of me that is. It was time to build on that foundation. It was time to be whole. Clear through.

Imprints

When I resolve into the essence

Which I most truly am

I feel a deep connection

With every living thing,

For That which most imbues me

With my identity

Is somehow in the other, too,

So that when I look around

I see myself – reflected.

Hidden in this union

Is the wonderful discovery

That if indeed the angels

May have wings –

Then so do I.

And if the essence of a flower

Drifts out on gentle breeze –

Then so do I.

And if the midnight sky

Is radiant with light –

Then so am I.

And if the silent mystery

Somehow becomes revealed

In tiny dew drops fair –

Then so am I,

For every lovely thing

Manifests the essence

That I am.

Oh beware, my soul, beware,

And move with gentle heart

Throughout this mystic veil

For if Love has left its imprint here –

Then so have I!

NINE

Pieces of the Puzzle

*"Go toward the things that are
calling you at your deepest levels."*

I did a lot of reading that summer. Whatever I could find on spirituality, health and healing, and, yes, even death and dying was fair game. While much of what I read wasn't new to me, it was what I needed to hear at that particular point in time. I needed to get back on track with all I knew to be right and true. Reading was like a ship's compass for me, guiding me to where I needed to be in my thinking.

I was like a sponge, devouring one book after another, making copious notes all the while. I felt as though I was taking intensive training in how to recover. "School" was definitely in session, and the benefits were enormous. New clarity emerged in my thinking, and a sense of rightness in my spirit.

I "remembered" even more when Marjorie and I went to Deepak Chopra's weeklong course on spirituality and the mind-body connection. The workshop was in Colorado, and it was like a healing salve for my soul. Not only were we immersed in the beauty of the mountains, we were also caught up in the incredible opportunity of simply being able to focus inwardly for an extended period of time. It was exactly what I needed.

Pure air, pure thought, pure fellowship, pure motive, pure energy can be truly transforming when entered into with an open, receptive heart. Daily we attended lectures and discussions on the deep issues of life. Threaded through all of this discourse were periods of meditation where we put our thoughts aside and just relaxed into the acute silence of our mountain setting. More and more the silence became a viable, almost palpable thing. It became a presence, a state, an indescribable, unforgettable aspect of ourselves as we released our cares and anxieties and simply allowed ourselves to be.

I was amazed at the difference this made. In the pure state of simply being, there are no problems. When I allowed myself to just *be*, I discovered that what I was, was enough. More than enough. There, away from all outer distraction, I was able to move into a higher level of awareness that lifted me up, much like a bird in flight. It was rather like having a wind in my spiritual sails that took me beyond all earthly complexities into a realm where all is complete, and all is whole, where harmony and beauty and love abide.

In this new place, I touched upon the part of me that lives in the heart of silence. As I became acquainted with that silent inner self, I experienced a total shift in the ground of my being. Where before I was wandering aimlessly on the seas of life, now I was anchored securely to my Source. Ignorance gave way at last to the light of understanding, and in that understanding, the purpose of my existence began to reveal itself. Confusion that had plagued me for so long just fell away into the nothing it truly is.

Once I experienced this inner domain, each moment became colored by this new reality that I had perceived. Suddenly, all was seen—and approached—in a new way. There was great energy here—dynamic, creative energy that reached into the very heart of things and transformed them and infused them with a deep and abiding sense of love. It was a total shift in focus, a complete change in approach. As this new way of being and doing grew within me, I found myself seeing things with new eyes.

The beauty of such an experience is that it lets you find your anchor. It lets you find the part of yourself that is totally unaffected by what happens around you. It lets you touch upon That which is unchanging in the midst of all that does change. This is why "going into the Silence," as it is called, is so satisfying. It allows you to touch upon the Infinite. When you do, you add a quality to your life that includes peace. From that peace comes the ability to face the things you cannot change—and that includes death.

Peace such as this moves you into a larger reality where there are no boundaries, no limits, and no unnecessary structure. It allows you to live and move in a state not governed so much by external constraints as by inner expansion, by a spiritual freedom to enter into an even greater sense of being-ness. When we find our spiritual center, even our work takes on new meaning. We sense a higher purpose that somehow brings a more unified quality to our daily living, even though we may not yet know what that purpose is. It seems sufficient simply to know that the purpose is there, that this is the journey that leads toward its realization.

Readers may wish to try Meditation #4 on finding your larger self, which is available in the Meditations section at the back of this book.

About the middle of the week, Deepak asked us to eat our lunch in silence. This was to be a time for reflection, even of communion. He told us ahead of time that there may be those who will cry, and if they do, we were told to enfold them lovingly in our prayers and continue with our meal. I remember thinking to myself, "Why would anyone *cry*?" It didn't take long to find out.

We got our lunch, sat down at our table, and began eating. As I ate, I thought about how amazing it was that I was actually there, doing what we were doing. Then suddenly it occurred to me, this is part of the gift! The gift that all things come bearing! The gift I'd walked and walked and walked trying to find! The realization took my breath away. The gift was so precious, but the cost had been so dear.

I began to cry. Not just cry, but weep. Not just weep, but sob—uncontrollably. And that's how I finished the lunch hour. Sitting there at the table sobbing. I never ate another bite. I just wept, totally overcome by the magnitude of the realization that Neal's passing had turned me toward the spiritual anchor I'd been searching for all my life. Feelings welled up within me I didn't know I had, and I left the noon hour filled with awe and wonder at what was transpiring in this magical place.

Two days later, we were sitting in our morning meditation when I noticed a light in the distance. My eyes were closed, so I was a bit puzzled as to how this could be. As I watched, the light drew a little closer. Curious, I moved a little closer, too. There seemed to be a magnetic pull coming from the light, as though it wanted me to move toward it. My curiosity seemed to encourage it, and as it drew closer still, I felt as though it was calling to me.

Suddenly, without knowing why, I felt an indescribable longing in my heart. More than anything, I wanted to be with that light, and I started pressing forward. As I did, the light moved toward me, too.

More and more my longing increased, so that all I wanted was to be closer to the light. A feeling of urgency grew within me and became so intense that I started rushing toward the light. As I did, my heart opened and my arms reached out to the light. Immediately, the light came forward and wrapped itself around me, enfolding me completely. As it did, I reached out and wrapped myself around it, too.

This was absolutely the most loving presence I have ever known, and it held me, and held me, and held me for as long as I wanted to be held. Instantly I knew it was the holding I had so longed for the day Neal had died, and yet it was even more than that. It was a holding that seemed to go back through all eternity, up through the present time, and far into the future, beyond anything I could see. It was a holding that went clear through to the roots of my being, and as it held me, I could feel us blending together.

In that divine embrace, all my pain and sorrow just drained away. All the heaviness in my heart evaporated so that all I knew in that eternal moment was love—complete, unqualified love. There was no sense of time, only one of deep, deep love, of being loved and accepted totally and completely by this presence, this light.

After what seemed like a very long time, I was able to release my hold. When I did, the presence ever so gently turned me around so I could see the world and all the people in it. It was all there in front of me, but off in the distance a little, and I could feel the arms of light around me as together we reached out to the world.

Then I heard, not audibly, but ever so clearly, "These are my beloved children in whom I am well pleased. Love them as I have loved you." When I heard that, I sensed that somehow they were my children, too, and that indeed I had been given a commission. I was to love them completely and without reservation. While I did not know how I was to do this, or what form that might take, I knew the answer would be revealed according to a plan I could not yet see.

After taking a moment to reflect on what had just happened, I turned to the light and immersed myself in it once more. Then, when my heart was truly filled, the voice said, "Go now, and I will be with you," and I returned in my awareness to the room where I had been sitting.

That window remained open to me for a full day and a half. Whenever I wished, I was allowed to move into the light, to be with the light, and walk and talk with it in my heart. It was as though I had one foot on earth doing what we were doing there at the workshop, and the other foot in this other dimension, simultaneously carrying on these conversations with this beautiful, loving presence.

Who can explain a moment such as this? Words are so inadequate. There is always so much that is left unsaid, but this much I know—we are never truly alone. More than that, we are cared for and watched over ever so tenderly, whether we know it or not. And, yes, we are loved with a love beyond anything words could ever portray. We are loved with a love so pure that in its presence, love is all there is. In that love, there is no scar, no blemish, not even anything to forgive. There is only light and acceptance and a love that flows out of the heart of Pure Being. We, too, are that love, for we are the product of that love. As we begin to remember this, so, too, will we begin to express it in our lives.

One cannot have an experience such as this without coming away changed, and so it was for me. Daily a feeling of inner expansion was with me, and because of it, I left for home with an inexplicable sense of purpose. Somehow, some way I was to share this peace and this love with others. I could only trust that how I was to do that would be made known in due time. Another piece to the puzzle had been found. I didn't know it then, but I was about to embark on a journey I did not even know I was seeking.

Oh Centered Candle

Oh centered candle, may I by thy light
Move my heart steadfastly toward thee.
Oh may thy light a beacon be
That I might find my life in thee.

When, in the dawn of each new day,
Thy light breaks forth upon my soul
So may I seek to find my way
And stumble not upon the shoal

That ever lurks near trembling feet
Which, pressing forth to grace the dawn,
Move with haste thy light to greet
While night's last tendrils linger on.

Oh gentle light, thou art my joy.
My every waking hour yearns for thee
Causing all effort to employ
That I might now more constant be.

Oh centered candle, lead me on
That I may rest my soul in thee
So when at last I reach the dawn
My spirit may be truly free.

TEN

Charting a New Path

"Adversity shapes and defines us in ways that nothing else can."

It surprises me now that I ever hesitated to attend the course in Colorado. The issue was the money. I'd never spent money like that on myself. Neal and I had taken a lot of wonderful trips, and I'll always be glad we did. However, it was another matter altogether to do that just for myself, so my thought when I got out there was, "You'd better enjoy this, because you'll probably never do it again!" That attitude soon changed.

There were well over six hundred people attending the course, with over twenty countries represented. There was a bank of interpreters that filled the three-sided balcony. People were speaking in languages I'd never heard before. When that many people get together to study and meditate, the energy can be palpable. It lifted us up so that by the time the week was over, we almost didn't need a plane to fly home.

About halfway through the course, Deepak started talking about the course on mind-body medicine they were offering in Chicago later that year. *Mind-body medicine!* I about leaped out of my chair. That was exactly what I had been looking for! The more he talked about it, the more I knew I had to go, so, of course, the old conversation began again. I rationalized by telling myself I'd just do this one more course, and then I would be done with it. After all, I didn't want to be foolish about how I used my resources.

The Chicago course was all I'd hoped for. In addition to Deepak, Dr. David Simon, the Medical Director and Co-founder of the Chopra Center, was there, along with Roger Gabriel, head of Teacher Certification for the Chopra Center. As if that wasn't enough, Dr. David Frawley spoke (Dr. Frawley is known the world over for his work with Ayurveda, Sanskrit, and the ancient scriptures), as did Dr. Bernie Siegel (renowned cancer specialist), and also Dr. Candace Pert (highly recognized for her research and book, *Molecules of Emotion, The Science Behind Mind-Body Medicine*).

Then Deepak talked about other courses they would be offering the following year. When he mentioned *Creating Health*, it rang my bell. How could I not do that? So I went—and learned about other courses. I'm sure you get the picture. While the courses were feeding me at my deepest roots, I always came away wanting more. Finally I just gave myself permission to follow my heart and go where it led me. It led to *Grow Younger, Live Longer*. That led to *SynchroDestiny*, and that led to *How to Know God*, which Deepak taught in India! The list just goes on and on. If they offered it, I went.

Of course, all this time I had not forgotten my initial question, "How can I help these kids?" Every once in a while, I'd get an idea, but every time I did, there seemed to be a hand in front of my face saying, "Not yet. Just wait. Be patient." It was frustrating, but since I wasn't getting a clear answer, I just kept doing what was bringing so much joy into my life.

Then one day I learned about Jonathan Goldman and his work with healing sound. It tied in so well with what I'd been studying that I went out to Colorado to study with him, too. Jonathan talked about how everything at its basic level is energy. When energy vibrates, it makes a sound. Even though the human ear can't always hear it, sound and vibration are at the root of everything that is manifest.

This principle tied in so well with what we were learning about the practice of Primordial Sound Meditation that Deepak taught us. PSM is a mantra-based practice. Just to clarify, mantras are made up of a word or words that are used for the effect of their sound and vibration. Most meditation practices keep your attention at the level of the mind, but the mantras we use in PSM are in the ancient language of Sanskrit, which is based on the sounds of the universe. What makes these mantras unique is that included in your mantra is the sound the universe was making at the time that you were born. The correct sound is determined by applying Vedic mathematics to your personal birth information. This astrological mathematical system comes from the Vedas, which are the oldest scriptures on the planet. That sound, then, is your personal vibration. Not only is it the sound your physiology resonates with, it is your own unique vibrational pattern. Just as we each have a unique thumbprint, we also have a unique energy pattern. That pattern supports and sustains our physiology.

Thus, when we think our mantra, we are actually re-tuning our system to its own innate pattern. I like to think of the mantra as our personal spiritual tuning fork. That re-tuning initiates the restoration of balance throughout our system.*

So now here I was with Jonathan, chanting, dancing, and meditating. Special rituals and ceremonies helped us move even deeper into the experience. It was beautiful.

The second time I studied with Jonathan, one ritual in particular stands out in my memory. Jim Albani, Jonathan's colleague and co-instructor, had us create three overlapping circles on the floor using dried corn. The formation is called the Tres Vesica. According to ancient legends, one circle represents heaven, another represents earth, and the third is for humanity. The symbology is that heaven represents God, but God needed a reflection, so he made earth. Then God needed a channel for expression, thus humanity was formed. As the circles overlap, one can see how body and spirit combine to form mind. Spirit and earth create the heart, while the earth and the body give birth to emotions. When all are in balance, we have unity.

The ritual was that sometime during our day of reflection we were to walk through the different places in the circular pattern and view our life from each perspective, until we reached the center. As I did this, I was overcome to see all the mistakes I'd made, the things I'd like to change, the times I've had to pick up

---

*To learn more about Primordial Sound Meditation, go to the Meditation page on www. DonnaMiesbach.com. If you'd like to find a teacher in your area, go to www.Chopra.com and click on "Find a Teacher." There are teachers all over the planet, so chances are you'll find one in your area.

the pieces and go on. It was all I could do to keep from falling apart completely.

As I walked through each of the sections, I thought about the significance they had in my life. I had no idea the ritual would be so powerful. After I retraced my steps, I found myself standing at the top looking down on myself through the eyes of our Creator. I felt such compassion and love, and absolute total acceptance. Again, I felt like crying, it touched me so deeply.

After a while I went over to my chair and sat down. As I sat there reflecting on what had just happened, I began to hear a Voice, and this is what it said:

> *My child, there is nothing to forgive. I seek only the full and free expression of My loving, creative Spirit through all My Creation, but only as it is able to receive it. I would not ask a child to carry a man's portion, and so with you, My beloved. Always I have understood your weaknesses. Always I have bolstered up your strengths. If need be, I would wait through all eternity for you to be ready to receive Me in the fullness which I desire to give unto you.*
>
> *Know this, then, My child, that you are never lost. Never did I not know your pain, your struggle, your sorrow. I have always been with you. You could not always see Me. You did not always hear Me, but I was there, so remember this, for in the days to come there will be times when you will wonder where I am. Do not despair. Look in your heart, for I will be there. Yea, I am there even now, and so it shall be through all eternity, for you are My beloved, and we have a journey to keep—you and I. It began long ago, before even time and space began, and it shall continue beyond even your furthest imagining, for I have a plan for you, My beloved. That plan will take you beyond the farthest stars, beyond even the distant galaxies to places of which you have not even dreamed where rivers and valleys sing for joy, and sorrow and sighing is no more, where all creation sings the wondrous rapture that is born from the pure joy of My Being, for it is in Me that you dwell, My child. In Me you live and move and have your being. Just as I am in your heart, so, too, are you in Mine. It could not be any other way.*
>
> *So come now. Let us walk the path together, for thus it has always been, and thus it shall always be. Amen, and Amen.*

ELEVEN

A Deeper Issue

*"Letting go opens our eyes to the
truth that nothing is ever really lost."*

That summer, I noticed a soreness in my left shoulder. At first I didn't think too much about it. I figured I'd probably swung the wrong way on the golf course, but by the time I got back from studying with Jonathan, it wasn't any better. In fact, it seemed worse.

I began to wonder if it was the onset of a "frozen shoulder." I'd had one on the other side about ten years before. Walking my hand up the wall had helped that time, but it didn't help this time. In fact, by September there was no denying that my shoulder was stuck. Oh, there was a little movement, but not much. It was time to get help.

Since the methods the therapist had given me before weren't working this time, I decided to try a different tack. I found a doctor who uses acupuncture along with cranial-sacral therapy. I'd read enough to know that sooner or later emotional stress takes its toll on the body. I figured the problem with the shoulder was a residual of all my grieving. I felt certain the therapy would take care of it and my shoulder would be back to normal once again. What I didn't know was the pain in my shoulder was just the tip of the iceberg.

The therapy did help. My shoulder began loosening up, and the pain was lessening, but there were still a couple of hot spots that were quite sore. When I mentioned them to Steve, my therapist, he began working on the tender areas. The next thing I knew I was crying, great heaving sobs like I had experienced in the early days of my grief. This came as a total surprise. Steve asked me why I was crying. I had to say I didn't know, and I didn't know, but for the next two days, every time I turned around it seemed I wanted to cry.

I knew I had to get to the bottom of what was going on, so finally I sat down to write out everything that was in my heart. I was amazed at what came out. Even though I thought I had worked through my grief very well, there was still a lot of unresolved "stuff" inside, such as the things I wished I'd had a chance to say or do before Neal died. It was still bothering me that I hadn't been there with him when he died when I had always been there for him. I agonized over the things I'd have done differently if I had known this was coming—like working less and playing more.

I wrote it all down, and with it came the startling revelation that I was still holding on. That stopped me right in my tracks. I thought I had dealt with this when Neal first visited me after he died. Obviously, there was a deeper issue here.

As I pondered all this, I began to wonder if my clinging was slowing down his own transition. Could it be that all my grieving was preventing Neal from making the most of where he was now? I didn't see how it could. Nevertheless, if there was even a remote possibility that it might be so, I certainly didn't want to do that. He didn't deserve that after all the wonderful years we'd had together.

I thought about that a lot over the next few days, and as I did, the image of an umbilical cord started surfacing in my mind. It seemed to represent the bond between us, the invisible connection that still felt so strong. There was a message here, but what was it trying to say?

Finally, it dawned on me that the cord that was connecting us needed to be cut. I had to let him go—completely—if ever he was going to be free to move along his new path. In my heart, I knew that was what I had to do. It was truly the only gift I had left to give him.

So one day I sat down in the privacy of our home and said my final goodbyes. I thanked him for all the years we had shared and told him it was all right now for him to go on. Even though I would miss him, I understood that this is how it needs to be for now. Then in my heart, I cut the cord. I let him go. It was a tearful time, but also a very tender time. It was the most loving thing I knew to do, so I did it.

I really expected that to be the end of it, but no sooner had I given the gift than I began to understand that this was exactly what Neal wanted for me, too! Just as much, he wanted me to be free to go on with my life, to explore my potential and do the things I needed to do to complete my time here. That hadn't occurred to me before, but instantly I knew it was right, and so, in that quiet, holy moment, we gave our gifts of love and freedom to each other.

That's when the "window" opened, and there he was, standing right before me, and he was magnificent. He was beautiful. He was healed. He was whole, and he was radiant. I don't know where we were, but we were in some other place, and I was seeing him as he is. More than that, I was allowed to see how it is for him over there now, and how it will be when we are together again. I was helped to understand even more clearly why it needs to be this way now, the wisdom behind it all, how the tie that bound us together on earth needed to be released so we could each be free to be our own self.

I saw, too, that there will always be a bond between us, but it is a bond of love that rejoices in the freedom of each other to become the magnificent being that has been patiently waiting to emerge. All this and more filled my heart and soul in that sacred moment.

When the window closed, I was at peace—completely at peace for the first time since he had died. It was all right, and I knew it was all right. He is all right. I am all right. Everything is all right. It was incredible.

My whole being was so filled with love and light and joy that I felt as though I could fly. My spirit soared. I literally felt as though there was nothing I couldn't do. In that moment my grief had been healed. My body was healed. My spirit was healed. The pain was gone. The weight that had always hung so heavily in my heart was gone. I felt so light. My spirit just sang. Joy came spilling out, and to this day I still marvel at the wonder of it. In giving my beloved the gift of freedom, we both were freed to be and do and go as we need to right where we are.

Never in my wildest dreams had I thought this would be possible. Never ever in my life did I think I could be so full of joy, but that is what happened, and it made all the difference. The change this made in my life was dramatic. In fact, it took me a while to get acquainted with this new, happy soul that kept masquerading as me. Sometimes I had to pinch myself to make sure I was really awake, that it wasn't just a dream. But I was awake, and it was me.

Deep in my heart I knew this incredible gift was meant to be shared, so I began writing my story in the hope that others might come to understand that while grief is a natural response to loss, you don't have to live with it forever. Indeed, it is not intended that we do, for all things do come bearing a gift. That gift is inherent in the lessons we learn as we work through the challenge that is presented to us.

Yes, it is possible to break through that last hurdle of grief and into the peace and joy that sorrow so completely crowds out. It is possible to discover, once and for all, the freedom and joy that come when we can love enough to finally, truly let go.

What Sweet Joy Is This

Tell me now -
Can you embrace the pain
Of mortal longing,
Can you welcome it
This day, this hour?
Can you run with it
And chase it wildly
So as not to miss
One moment of its
Exquisite suffering?

What sweet joy is this
That moves beyond
All sorrow
Until even the pain
Is changed
To dancing?

TWELVE

Letting Go

*"Victories of the spirit require—indeed,
demand—letting go of things as they were."*

Letting go begins a healing that can only occur deep within us. Letting go means letting go of the old and embracing the new. It means being willing to go forward—anyway. It means recognizing that life continues, even in the midst of change.

Letting go brings you right into the present moment. That means confronting the *space*. It means looking ahead, so you can go on with your life—as it is. Once you are willing to do this, you develop a spaciousness in your thinking that opens you to the realm of possibility, the domain of your potential. Letting go brings you back to life and living. It broadens your perspective so you can see where you are and what still needs to be done. This makes it easier to face your issues honestly and then learn from them.

When you do finally get to this point, you are on the brink of freedom. We live with sorrow until we are willing to let go of it, until we are ready to get on with life and living. We have to find out that it's okay to be okay. Joy is not a denial of the loss, as I once thought, but rather a confirmation of the quality of the relationship we had. Because our relationship with our beloved was so special, we are now able to go on.

Grief creeps into our lives in so many ways. Friends or family move away, children grow up and leave home, jobs change, pets die, a treasured possession becomes damaged or lost. One of the reasons these changes are so difficult is because they link us to what we know and are comfortable with. Those emotional connections are links to the past.

I have often wondered, if given the chance, would we choose to always live our lives in the past and never in the present? It would be unfortunate if we did, for it is only in the present that our truest joys can be found. It is only in the present moment that we most fully experience the peaks—and, yes, the valleys—of life.

This being so, then why is it so difficult to be here—to be here *now*? Perhaps it is simply a matter of habit. Are we "programmed" to walk through life with our proverbial head on backward, looking at where we have been? That is what grief is, you know—a backward glance. As I sit here working on my computer—my word processor—it occurs to me that perhaps we are *experience* processors, and indeed this we must be if we are ever to make sense out of, or find the meaning and value in, our experiences. The trick is not to get stuck in the past.

Once we have made our evaluation, once we have made peace with the issue, then we must be willing to let go. We must be willing to move on. Of course, to actually do that, we have to let go of how things were. We have to let go of how we would like things to be. In other words, we have to be willing to let go of what we cannot change.

Letting go proved to be incremental to my healing. Until I was able to do that, I was bound to the past. I could not move forward. I had to put both feet in the boat before it could take me where I needed to go. Letting go meant putting both feet in the boat. It meant accepting the inherent lesson and then moving forward on the strength of what I had learned.

It is impossible to describe the difference letting go makes. Suffice it to say it leads to the ultimate healing, for with it comes freedom such as you have never known before. With it comes a joy beyond description. With it comes a peace that surpasses by far all the grief you have experienced.

> **Readers may wish to try Meditation #2 on letting go, which is available in the Meditations section at the back of this book.**

The interesting thing is that the gifts letting go brings affect all involved. The repercussions don't stop just with you. They reach out into every area of your life, and that includes all those whom your life touches. The changes in you that are brought on by this "simple" act of letting go radiate out into your life much like ripples on a pond. Everything is touched by it—by the very magic of it—in one way or another. You meet life differently. Others notice it. You do, too. Since you can't explain it, you find yourself content to simply let it be what it needs to be—in you, through you. Somehow that seems to be enough.

You see, once your resistance is gone, once acceptance has entered your heart, the "negative" side of the experience becomes transformed into what some might call a positive thrust forward. That is exactly what happens. Your increased understanding, your deepened insight, equips you with new coping tools that alter forever how you meet the events of life. It allows you to come from a broader, more compassionate perspective. It allows you the freedom to more fully be yourself. In this new way of being, you are able to reach out in ways you had not thought of before. Those simple acts of caring bring healing to all your life touches.

We are such a vast sea of humanity. I have often wondered, and no doubt you have, too, what difference one person can make. If you are wondering about this, try putting a drop of ink into a bowl of water and see what happens. The ink spreads, doesn't it? *All* the water changes color. That's a rather simple way of describing what I am talking about, but it is a good analogy, because when you are healed, I am healed, and when you suffer, we all suffer.

In one way or another, and to one extent or another, we do indeed share our common lot. Whether we know it or not. Even whether we want to or not. As the old adage says, when one strand shakes, the whole web trembles. That is why every bit of courage you muster is just that much more courage for all of us. Every time you find a way to triumph over the challenges of life, our spirit is elevated that much more. As you discover and grow into your finest self, so do we all.

I am reminded of mountain climbers going up the side of a mountain, each one connected to the other through the lifeline, the rope that ties them together. When one is safe, when one is secure, they all are. When one is in danger, they all are. We are a lot like that, I think, and therein lies a responsibility that cannot be denied, for as we search for our highest and best, it is not just we alone who will benefit. Every bit of progress you make means just that much more progress for us all.

While it is true that such lofty goals are rarely at the front of our thinking when we are faced with great challenge, it can be fortifying to know it is not for ourselves alone that we struggle. It is not just for ourselves that we seek light to guide us. We are *all* searching, even when we least know it. When I am at my weakest, you may be at your strongest. When you are beset with difficulties, there will be others who are "feeding the pump." It matters not when or who, for we are in this together. While we each must meet our own challenges, it is together that we will triumph.

May It Never Be Said

May I bring you gifts
Of joy and laughter
To nourish your spirit
And unleash the tethers
Of all your longings
So you may dance
In both sunlight and shadow
And sing in your darkest hour.
Oh may it never be said
When I leave this earth
That I did not love you enough!

THIRTEEN

This Rich Gift

*"Acceptance gives you the perspective
to see what you can or cannot change."*

There is an old saying that things tend to come in threes. I certainly never expected that to be the case with regard to death in our family, but that is exactly what happened three and a half years after Neal's sudden death.

Mother and Daddy loved to travel. After Daddy retired, it became their pastime, but this time Mother hadn't been feeling well. Since Daddy really wanted to visit Australia and New Zealand again, she mustered up all the energy she could find and off they went.

When it was time to meet their return flight, I expected it to be like all the other times. I thought about how good it would be to see them, how much fun we would have talking about what they had done, but a happy homecoming was not to be. This time it was different.

This time when I met them at the airport, I learned that Mother had had heart problems almost the entire time they were gone. She spent most of the trip praying nothing would happen to her before they got home. Daddy, on the other hand, had been very well, but the day they flew home he became ill. Two days later they were both in the hospital.

The doctors were able to help Mother's problem for a while. Daddy, however, had picked up a strain of pneumonia that was not included in the vaccine we use here in this country. The doctors said he may have caught it from some sheep they were near just before they flew home from New Zealand. Pneumonia makes a terrible assault on the body. For someone at the age of ninety, its threat can be even greater.

Mother was frantic. Being in another part of the hospital, she was unable to be with Daddy, to help him and comfort him. Fortunately, she was released after the third day, and thus it was that our vigil began.

It is said that all things come when you are ready. Was I ready to lose my parents? Certainly I did not think so, and yet there we were, pondering the outcome of this unexpected turn of events. With each passing day, it became more and more obvious that they were preparing for their final journey together, a journey that would take them to a place where I could not meet them for what no doubt would seem like a very long time.

I have often heard that when someone brings something into your life, it is because there is something they need of you. Their need is, in turn, their gift to you, because what you are required to give provides an opportunity to reach into yourself in a way that otherwise you would not have had.

In fact, I referred to this very concept in a manuscript I was completing as my parents were returning from their trip abroad. In it I talked about how love sees us through all the phases of life, and through death as well. I discussed the gift that all things come bearing. I also looked at ways of approaching challenge— like asking yourself, *What is this trying to teach me?* and *How is this helping me grow?*

It seemed strange, as I stood there in the Emergency Room, and later in Intensive Care, and later still in the weeks that followed, to be asking myself the very questions I had just been writing about. Yet at that time and in that hour, there was nothing to do except ponder them.

The importance of preparing for the tough times had never seemed truer than now. My premise that there is much we can do to shore up the weak places and strengthen our spiritual sinews ahead of time was indeed shown to be true during all those difficult hours. I couldn't help thinking back just three and a half short years to Neal's passing—how far I had come, how much I had learned, and how it had helped prepare me for yet another difficult period in my life.

Would that I had known then what I knew now! Perhaps the trauma of Neal's death would not have been so all-consuming, and yet in retrospect it seemed that even that was one of his gifts to me, for out of it was born the fruit of understanding on which I now depended so heavily.

I had always prayed that when the time came, death would be easy for my loved ones. This was far from easy—for them or for me. Why were they doing it this way? Was there some aspect of life they still wanted to experience? Was my father's strong desire to make this trip an intuition of a divine appointment he needed to keep? Was there some special gift they were offering before they took their leave? The questions presented themselves over and over to me as we moved through the many stages of this experience.

In spite of his suffering, Daddy's final weeks unfolded into a beautiful tapestry of gifts given and received, an inner weaving of our souls that was composed of love's finest gossamer. Much of the time it happened in unexpected ways.

One night when I was in the twilight between waking and sleeping, I found myself holding Daddy's hand. He must have called to me, for there I was. Even though I was a full fifteen-minute drive away from him, in our spirits we were together, and I was holding his hand just as I did at the hospital, sending him all the love and strength I could. At one point I turned to Mother, thinking she might need comforting, too, but she was not there, so Daddy and I shared the moment quietly together. Words were never spoken, but volumes were said within our hearts.

At other times the words "This is my body which is broken for you" (I Corinthians 11:24) kept floating up to the surface of my mind. I could not ponder its meaning without being overcome both by tears and awe. More and more I became aware of the extravagant gift being bestowed upon me—by Daddy, by our

Creator whose Spirit most certainly inhabits these bodies, and certainly by Mother, for surely at some level she must have agreed to participate in this charade.

So why was such a rich gift being given? The pain and suffering, the lingering and sorrow, and, yes, even the fear these two dear ones shared comprised the varied threads of this elegant tapestry. After their many years together, the end was drawing near, and they were not yet ready to say goodbye. Nor was I.

In their most unselfish way, they were giving me the opportunity to plumb depths of love that previously I'd been unable to reach. Perhaps it had not been accessible to me before. Was it the growth I had made since my husband's death that opened me to this deeper form of love? If this were true, then even that growth had been Neal's gift to me, at least in part. Now Mother and Daddy were giving me the opportunity to practice what I had come to understand. Yes, it was indeed time to move into deeper levels of living, not only to explore but perhaps even to master that which I had come to see as truth.

We cannot share what we do not know, and we cannot know what we have not experienced. Believing and knowing are not the same. Belief is an assumption based on understanding. Knowing is more than that. It is knowledge based on experience, and it flows from our deepest springs. It resonates with the truth of our being. So it was that all the things I had been learning came into play—things like the need for humor to bolster the spirit and lighten the moment and, even more importantly, the ability to move into the silent spaces and rest in the peace that can only be found within us.

Over and over I saw with ever greater clarity the importance of what I had been saying to grief groups about developing our coping skills ahead of time. Now it was being proven in my own experience. As I said many times, the best time to learn to swim is before you fall overboard. Once you are in choppy water, you already need to know how to keep afloat, to do your strokes, to breathe properly, all the things that make for good swimming. Choppy seas are never a good place to learn survival techniques. It is just as true of life, although sometimes that is exactly what we must do.

Certainly my studies helped bring me to this place in my understanding. The resulting growth from all the introspection and meditation allowed me to meet this new challenge with different eyes and a less fearful heart. In retrospect I believe it was the practice of meditation that contributed the most to my spiritual grounding. It taught me how to move away from outer turmoil into my peaceful center, away from the questions to where the answers are.

In meditation we learn to connect with that Still Point deep within us where all is well even when nothing seems to be well. Yet if we have never done this, it is extremely difficult to find that quiet place when we are in crisis. We need to have done our homework. We need to have developed the skill, to have practiced it in little things, so we can be adept when big issues arise.

Readers may wish to try Meditation #5 on the breath, which is available in the Meditations section at the back of this book.

Meditation is such an important coping tool. It connects you to your deep center, the part of you that is never sick, that is not afraid, that does not die. It allows you to move into the part of you that is, regardless. I did not have this tool when Neal died. I was acquainted with meditation, but not practiced in it. The investment I had made in its practice since his death proved to be more valuable than I ever would have expected, for now here I was, moving through the final chapter of my parents' lives, and we were meeting it with love, not fear. I was facing it with a compassion that could only come from the trust that was grounded deep within me. It brought an "other" quality to the whole experience, which enabled us to explore this rich gift of life as we shared it together, day by precious day.

That is what life is, of course—a very rich gift. As we learn to go within ourselves, as we move toward our deep, spiritual center, we are allowed to explore the many facets that life presents. That opportunity is an invitation that speaks to our deepest yearning and ultimately satisfies the hunger within us. As we fathom these bottomless deeps, we touch upon the very wellspring of creation itself. Where the act of creation is, there too is the Creator. That statement is truer than we know, and it was soon to prove itself in ways I never could have imagined.

In the weeks that followed, the phrase "midwife to the dying" kept floating into the perimeter of my mind. I knew where it had come from. It was how Joan Halifax, a well-known author, teacher, and medical anthropologist, described her hospice work in Susan Skog's book, *Embracing Our Essence, Spiritual Conversations with Prominent Women*. While I liked the concept, I never dreamed I would soon be doing that, too.

And so it was that as I watched all the ups and downs of Daddy's illness, in my heart I wondered if this was part of a birthing process, or would he actually get well? Were these steps toward his release from his body or his efforts to remain in it? Were we unknowingly assisting him in his entry into another level of life?

Then I would think of Mother, how she fluttered around him, a ministering angel if ever there was one. Did she know, somewhere in the deep recesses of her being, that their time together on this plane was coming to a close? Were these gentle, tender acts of kindness her only remaining gifts to give him?

That picture is indelibly etched in my memory. In a way, we were participating in it, too, comforting him, hovering over him, tending to his needs out of the vast reservoir of love and concern we felt for him. Little did we know, on the conscious level at least, that we were helping him prepare for his final voyage from this place.

FOURTEEN

How to Gaze Upon the Stars

*"When we truly listen, the silence leaves spaces within us
that are just as vibrant, just as quiet, just as immense
as that which inspired them."*

Daddy and I loved to watch the night sky. Some of my earliest memories go back to doing that with him. Even as a child, it captured my imagination and set me to pondering unanswerable questions.

Star gazing speaks to the hidden spaces in our soul, and creates an unutterable longing for keys to the mysteries of the universe, keys that we hope will also unlock secret places deep within us. There is something about the stars that seems to tell us we are just as grand, that there is something just as immense inside us. The link is sensed, the connection is felt, but the questions remain.

There are probably as many ways to gaze upon the stars as there are people. Ask anyone. They will tell you, but their answers will all be different. Away from city lights, they will say. Out in the country, they will answer. From a mountain top. The plains. The deeps of a valley. Through a telescope. The point of view depends on where the person is. Of course. But there is one way that is by far the best of all—through the eyes of a child, while holding your father's hand.

This is not to say it can happen anytime one is a child. No, I would not want to imply that, for not just any age will do. To be too old or too young would be to miss the wonder. The moment belongs to the age of innocence, before wisdom and knowledge can cloud the reason. Yes, it has to be when the child is ripe with wonder, like an apple so full of its wonderful juices that it can no longer hang on the bough. It has to be a moment like that, when the eyes are wide and trusting and the heart is able to perceive the magic that only a child can recognize.

You have to choose your season, too, for to do it in the midst of winter is to be distracted by the cold. True, stars are bright and clear in winter, but the concentration is disturbed by the need to stay warm, to not be outside too long. The wind tugs hard at the muffler wrapped around your face, and hands seek the lingering warmth of down-protected pockets. Yes, it is hard to lose yourself in magnificence when your extremities are getting numb.

Neither would spring be best, for that is when the juices all begin to flow. The tremor of new life is in the air, and all around you things are happening. It is hard to be still when Nature's exuberant activity surrounds you. When you can actually stand there and hear the pine trees popping their cones. When you can feel the new grasses pushing up from the ground, and more sense than smell the fervor of spring's excitement upon the gentle breeze. No, there is too much to think about to try to stand and gaze at the stars in the spring.

The same is true of autumn, for that is the other end of the cycle. Things are winding down. The whole process is coming 'round full circle. Musty leaves send up their pungent odor, and the smell of crackling bonfires is in the air. The edge of winter nips at your imagination, and overhead the restless call of birds disturbs the chance for peaceful contemplation of silent mysteries.

Yes, it would have to be summer. It would have to be a warm summer's night, when the world is still, and the birds are asleep, and you would be, too, were it not for the fact that your father has something to show you. Rarely are you up this late, so you know it must be special. You know it has to be something worthy of so great an exception.

When the sun goes down after so long a day—far longer than any other time of year, the darkness is that slow in coming—that makes it very late indeed, especially when you are so young. Yes, that is most unusual. Nor could it be just any father. No, it needs to be someone who has shared his lap with you. Someone who has tossed pennies in the ring with you. Someone who has taken you into his workshop and called you "Chief" as you helped him with his projects. Someone who made you feel special, even though you were only seven.

When you have that kind of father, it makes staying up late even more important. It makes the anticipation all the more exciting, so that when the dark finally does come and he takes you by the hand, you know this is truly a moment of moments. This is something you will not forget, so out you go together, hand in hand, and he shows you. He tips your face up to the sky, and you see them. Like great, luminescent pearls in the vast vault of heaven, they hang there, and you know they are just for you. Just for the two of you. And so you look, not even wanting to speak, just letting your soul feel the immensity that would somehow overwhelm you, but for your father's hand.

Then, after a while, after you have made friends with the silence, and the stars, and the mystery, he tells you the ancient legends. He shares their secrets with you. He unscrambles the puzzle for you, so that out of all that myriad of blinking stars figures appear. The Big and Little Dippers. The North Star. Orion and the Pleiades. The planets. The Milky Way. He tells you how they have guided man since time began, and somehow you know that they will always be there, that they will guide you, too. It's a holy moment. A moment only a child can experience, only a child can understand.

In that moment, you know that once he was a child, too. That once upon a time someone took him by the hand, and somehow you feel connected to the mystery that man has shared since his conception. Even though you don't yet know the answers, you realize you have tasted just a little of the questions, and in that realization you know you are special. You know he knows it, too, and somewhere in the private corners of your heart, you tuck the memory away. You keep it with the treasures that can only be kept within you, so that even though the days may pass and the years may flee away, deep inside you is the knowledge that once upon a time you gazed upon the stars, and they belonged to you.

Traces of the Infinite

Was that a shooting star I saw
There on the horizon
Or a momentary glimpse
Of the sweeping hand of God,
Leaving in its wake
Traces of the infinite?

Sometimes I think I see
That same hand at work
Within our lives
When doubt grows into faith
And blossoms into love,
Leaving trails of stardust
In our hearts.

FIFTEEN

A Lesson in Courage

*"Our most difficult challenges nearly
always are our most important teachers."*

The Missouri River has always played a rather large part in my life. Not only did I grow up near it, but my father spent his entire working career bringing that river under control. The objectives were to prevent future flooding and to make the river navigable. It took thirty-seven years, but Daddy got the job done. More than once, as I was growing up, I referred to it as "my Daddy's river." To me it still is.

That is probably why I found the book *Undaunted Courage* by Stephen E. Ambrose so interesting. It is the story of the expedition Lewis and Clark made up that same river. It was an incredible journey, one that began when our country was only twenty-seven years old! President Thomas Jefferson hand-chose Meriwether Lewis for the job, and Lewis in turn hand-picked William Clark to assist him. I marvel that Jefferson would have so much vision at a time when our country was so young.

What Jefferson wanted to do, among other things, was find a waterway via the Missouri River to the Pacific Ocean. He was hoping the Missouri River would connect with the Columbia River, thus providing an important artery for expansion and commerce.

But that wasn't all. He asked Lewis to make as complete a map as possible of their journey. He wanted Lewis to make a thorough study of the flora and fauna wherever he went. He wanted to know the condition of the soil, what the land and the climate were like, where the natives were, what they were like, and a record of their languages. And there was more. Much more.

In short, since Lewis was going where no white person was known to have gone before, Jefferson wanted to know everything Lewis could tell him about the rest of North America. Lewis spent years just learning how to do all the things Jefferson hoped for, while Jefferson taught him, playing the part of a mentor in every sense of the word. It is amazing, considering how primitive their lives were, that Lewis succeeded in every way save one, and he was surely not to be faulted for that. The waterway simply did not exist. It was a huge disappointment, even though much had been learned about this previously unknown territory.

There were surprises every step of the way. It was thrilling for them to see creatures not yet known to exist, to discover new kinds of vegetation, unusual land forms, breathtaking scenery, but their days were incredibly difficult. Impossible terrain. Everything from huge mosquitoes to mile after mile of cactus to walk through with only simple moccasins on their feet. Intense heat. Subzero temperatures. Not to mention the seemingly endless Rocky Mountains. They endured it all.

Lewis knew ahead of time that the mountains were nearly impassable, but that didn't stop him. He reasoned that if the Indians could find a way through, they could, too. I can't imagine having to climb those rugged cliffs in the middle of winter, let alone having to struggle with faltering horses on the steep and narrow passes. Over and over they had to stop and regroup so they wouldn't lose their precious supplies. Food was scarce, the opportunity for rest almost nonexistent. The difficulties they encountered were enormous, but Lewis's unfaltering confidence kept the men going, regardless. His attitude made all the difference.

Attitude is always the key, isn't it? Moving into unknown territory is never easy, no matter what you're facing, but our biggest challenge is always within us. What we bring to life makes all the difference. I was seeing that now, too, as I watched Daddy go through his final illness. Even though his life-breath was being taken away from him day by day, his amazing courage and fortitude set an example for us all.

I saw how we are all explorers, how we continually move into territory where we've never been before. I saw, too, how our experience of life really is in our hands. I say that because, regardless of what happens around us, what happens inside us is ours to govern. It's ours to control. That's where life happens—inside us, and that is what Daddy was showing me. He'd always been my teacher, and he still was. He was meeting what life brought him with the same integrity that had been his standard for ninety years.

Having courage does not prevent our ship from being buffeted by the storms of life. The storms are still going to come. It's what we do when the storms hit that is going to make the difference. We may have to "go with the wind" for a while. We may have to let events take us where they will until we can get a firmer grip on things, but if we know it is up to us to bring ourselves back in balance, we'll have a lot better chance of righting our ship and getting on with our life.

While that may be easier said than done, it is possible. It's possible because we already have what we need within us. It just may take some doing to find it. Meeting the storms of life requires a willingness to defy our fear and a refusal to be shaken. It means being tenacious in our determination to bring the best out of a situation, an unwillingness to settle for anything less. And, yes, it takes a strength of mind bordering on fearlessness to sail in troubled waters and come through stronger for the effort it required.

Actually, strength and endurance are intrinsic parts of our deep spiritual nature. They were infused into our being before we ever came here, and they are born into our conscious experience through the simple act of trusting. Of knowing. Of being at peace in your deep center when everything around you seems to be in a state of chaos.

Peace is purely an inward occurrence. It doesn't do any good to wait for "things" to settle down, because "things" aren't going to settle down until we do. Peace doesn't happen outside us until it happens within us. That is why our work always needs to begin within. We need to explore our spiritual depths. We need to get acquainted with our deep spiritual center. We need to know how to move into our silent interior where everything is all right even when nothing seems to be all right. When we can do that, our fear dissolves into the nothingness that it truly is, for we have found the peace that truly is beyond all understanding. The peace that tells us that all is well. The peace that knows what cannot be put into words.

From this holy place, courage is born—courage that knows— courage that trusts—courage that has as its foundation an understanding that goes beyond even understanding itself. When we can do this, we have begun to explore our inner terrain. There we discover the Self of us, which is far grander than we could imagine. That Self is the part of us that is. It is Who We Are. When we find that Self, we also begin to discover what we may yet become. Coming from this perspective, courage is not such a difficult commodity to come by after all, for this is a journey of the soul, and where that will take us, we have not even begun to dream.

Too soon the fateful day arrived. It was about five in the morning when I was awakened by the message: **HELP MY WILMA**. I could see the words in front of me, and they were in Daddy's printing. Immediately I knew he was asking me to help my mother and I answered, "Oh, Daddy, I will!" But what was going on? Had a decision been made? Was it time for him to go Home?

Finally I got back to sleep, only to find myself in the presence of a glorious being of light, and that being was healing the multitudes. There are some things for which there are no words. This was one of those things, for while I will never forget the magnificence of what I saw, there is no way to describe it. I just stood there watching, marveling, and thinking, *So this is how it's done!* It was almost as though I was being given a lesson on how to heal, as though I was being allowed to look light years ahead into our spiritual evolution when we, too, might render that same inestimable service.

As I watched, I felt I was being asked to send Daddy special healing energy, and I began doing so right away. Here again we were exchanging our priceless gifts—mine the gift of healing, his the opportunity for me to use it. I wondered if Daddy would be better when we got to the hospital, or was this the ultimate healing that death brings? There was no doubt in my mind that in some special way I was being allowed to assist in the process, whichever form it took. Truly, it was a pivotal moment, far more than I realized, for I had hardly awakened from the dream when the phone rang. It was the hospital telling us to come right away. They didn't tell us then, but he was gone.

No Longer Than a Glance

Dearest Heart,
I would not leave thee.
Never would I choose
To have our life-paths part.
The price of age sometimes
Is more than I can bear
And yet, my love, I know
That when we leave this earthly plane
It is just a moment, love,
A blink within eternity,
Before we meet again –
No longer than a glance is all
Before I see your face
Upon that joyful other shore
Where, holding out your hand to me,
You help me through the door.

SIXTEEN

Reverie

*"Love's way is all we could ever have
hoped for, all we could have asked."*

Daddy had always been so well. It was hard to believe he was gone. Each day it seemed as though it had never happened, and yet it had. We were always so close. We still are. Somehow that has not changed. At some deep level, we are still connected.

I believe this is true for all of us. We are all so much a part of each other—much more than we can possibly know during the time we dwell here. We glimpse that closeness through our parents, our children, and our loved ones, but it is no less with you and me, for are we not all formed out of the same spirit? Are we not all cut out of the same cloth?

I had such a strong sense of that after my husband died. That sense is even stronger now that Daddy is gone. It is as though part of me is here, and part of me is there. It was always that way, I think. It was that way when I came into this earth, and it will probably be that way when it is time for me to leave this human form, but there is a constant factor through it all. That factor is the love that supports and sustains us, wherever we are, however we are.

That love is the one unalterable certainty. It was the substance out of which we were formed, and the essence to which we will return. To have touched upon it is to know it is also our constant source of joy—joy to be found through the gifts we share, joy to be found through the very act of being itself. In that joy, there is no sorrow, only love.

And so it was that we shared our gifts, each of us resonating from our deepest springs. We fathomed depths of love that only the purest of intentions can reach. As we did, I learned to move beyond myself in an altogether different way. All that mattered was the reaching out, the supporting, the sustaining, the exchange between our souls.

These moments of love, these steps of compassion, this outpouring from being to being—what a pure form of existence it is! To assist someone through the final stages of life is a gift that is priceless beyond measure. At that time and in that hour, I was allowed to help Daddy move through a door that only the soul can enter. What could be more important than this?

Come, Gather Freely

Here, take my candle,
For I would not have you
Walking in darkness.
Take my shawl
For I do not want you
Shivering in the cold.
Take my bread
That it may give you
Strength for the journey.
Yes, and take my love
So you will never
Feel alone.
Take it all,
For your peace is as
A healing stream to me.
Your comfort echoes
In the chambers of my heart,
And your freedom is as
A light unto my very soul;
So come, gather freely,
For when you have
Found your way,
I, too, shall be
Made whole.

SEVENTEEN

Ministering to an Angel

"The bottom line is—it's about love. It's always about love."

Mother was frantic after Daddy died. There was so much to do, so little time. I didn't understand why she felt so driven. Why did she feel she had to make every minute count? Did she know what was about to transpire?

The days were full. We worked until noon answering mail, making phone calls, trying to get her affairs in order. Then we broke for lunch. After lunch the mail came, and we began all over again, but what was driving her to clear the boards, to tie up loose ends at such a frantic pace?

Often after Daddy was gone, Mother would say she didn't think she could be here without him. I don't believe it was intended that she should. They came here to be together. She started dating him when she was sixteen. They married when she was eighteen. It was the beginning of a wonderful lifetime together, so it didn't surprise us that Mother would follow Daddy in death. We just expected it to happen. What surprised us was how she did it. Her final illness was a journey none of us could have anticipated.

It began six weeks after Daddy died. Mother was having a particularly difficult day, so I took her to see a funny movie, hoping it would help a little. It was good to sit and laugh together, but on the way home, her tears returned. After sixty-seven years of being together, separation was almost more than she could bear, so we sat in her kitchen and visited for a while before I walked home.

It was so convenient, living next door. Thirty seconds and I could be there. Many times I was. After about an hour I wondered if I should call and check on her. Just as I was having the thought, the phone rang.

"Donna, I'm on the floor and I can't get up."

I flew next door and found her on the floor in the bedroom. Sure enough, she had had a massive stroke. Somehow she had managed to drag herself to the phone and call me.

As I watched the paramedics work with her, again the thought, "This is my body, which is broken for you," (I Cor. 11:24) surfaced in my mind, and my heart cried out, "By *why*, Lord? Why this way? Why *her*?"

As vital and alive as Mother had always been, it never occurred to me that she would have to finish her life in a nursing home, but that's exactly what happened. So here we were at Chapter Two. Or was it Chapter Three? I wasn't sure. All I knew was that this dear lady whom we all adored was suddenly paralyzed and could not help herself. How quickly the roles are changed! After all her years of being here for us, now we were ministering to her, helping her through her final days.

It was just too much. She was tired, more tired than words could begin to express. As I stood by her bed one evening watching her drift into a deep sleep, the realization came over me that she was dying. Slowly—yes. By inches—yes, but she was surely dying. Gradually she was drifting away from the pain, away from the sorrow and grief, away from all she had known and loved here as she moved toward that which her heart now deeply desired—rest, peace, freedom from these mortal bonds, and most certainly to be with Daddy once again.

I could not begrudge her that. In fact, I wanted it for her. I loved her too much to ask for it to be any other way. We'd had our time together here, and it had been good. Very good. We both knew it, and we both had said so. The years had been rich indeed, and we were grateful. Now it was time for her to move on.

Much to our surprise, death did not come. In fact, after a steady six-month decline, suddenly her condition leveled off. She had reached a plateau of sorts, and a new experience opened up before us, one we could not possibly have imagined. Mother had moved into another space—a happy space—where she could see those who had gone on before her. Daddy was there, as was my aunt, and my grandmother—both long gone, but they were there, and they were with Mother. We could only sit in awe and watch the transformation as Mother's grief and sorrow were replaced by a radiant joy that illumined her beautiful face.

Our minister saw it, too. "She's on a bridge," she told me, "and she's deciding whether or not to cross it." Then she went on to explain that Mother was finishing her life cycle, completing her last task—the task of teaching us—*showing* us—how to bring life to a close with grace and peace.

The minister's words certainly helped answer some of the questions I'd been pondering about how Mother could be so cheerful when her husband, her body functions, and now even her home were gone. Mother could see beyond all that, and in her own gentle way, she was showing us that "things" are not so important after all. It was all right. There is more to life than that.

All Mother had left to give was love, and she did so lavishly. Nothing else mattered. Only the love, the being together, the memories shared and cherished. It was evident that in her own way, Mother was ministering to us, even as we to her. Thus the circle became complete. All was well, even when nothing appeared to be well at all.

As the weeks went by, we watched Mother move back and forth between dimensions. Even though part of her was "there," she was perfectly capable of being with us here, too. Her mind was still sharp. She could relate the history of all the prominent tennis players. She could carry on lucid conversations about the decisions I needed to make regarding her finances. She knew who everyone was and had delightful conversations with her visitors. She even challenged the staff minister about some of the things he said in his weekly sermons, but at the same time, "they" were there. "They" were with her, and because they were, she was happy. She was content. A door had opened—not completely perhaps—but it was enough. She wasn't alone any longer.

Even though the weeks were so very difficult, I was grateful for the gifts they gave us—precious moments when we could express our love to each other, when I could reach out to her and tenderly caress her, and hold her in my arms and rock her much like she rocked me when I was a child. Sudden death does not bequeath such a legacy. Lingering death does. Perhaps that was part of the gift she was offering—this final, precious opportunity to affirm our love for each other, to acknowledge that all was as it should be, just as all will be as it should be even after she is gone.

After the minister told us Mother was on a bridge, I called the children, and they all came. We needed to be together now more than ever. It was a happy time, filled with love and laughter. As sick as she was, Mother loved every minute. In fact, she loved it so much, she decided not to leave. She wasn't ready to say goodbye.

When I asked the minister about this, she said, "She still wants to be your mother." Indeed! But what a price to pay! What a gift to offer, that she would willingly continue in this condition just so she could be with us! It boggled my mind just to think of it, yet that is exactly what was happening.

Later, when her condition was a little better, I asked her about it, and she confirmed what I had been told. "I just don't want to leave you," was her tender reply, but the day would come. We both knew that. We were acutely aware that our time together was not to be squandered. Each day was a gift that had been dearly bought. It should be just as dearly treasured. Even though Daddy had been with us for all those years, his departure came much too soon. No doubt it would seem the same with Mother, too.

The memories of Daddy's last days came streaming back to me with new poignancy, reminding me once again how there really are no endings. There are only new beginnings. We slip away from the old. We ease into the new. Gradually we let go. There is a grace about a death such as theirs, but then they were gracious in life. Why would it be any different in death? They did not rush but rather slowly took their leave, giving all a chance to say goodbye. Each gentle touch was a memory in itself, each twinkling smile a priceless gift to treasure.

It is hard to watch dear ones slowly take their leave, but then it was hard to lose my beloved husband so suddenly. There just is no easy way to do it. Either way leaves its questions to answer. Certainly I pondered many of those questions when I lost Neal. There were even more as Daddy lay dying. Then to be going through it again so soon with Mother, I could not help but wonder: What is there yet to glean from this? What is there yet to learn? Is she doing it this way to give me one last opportunity to stretch my spiritual muscles? It was almost as though I could hear her saying, "Reach a little deeper, Donna. There is more to understand. There is yet more you can become."

There is no question she was challenging me to tap the deep resources of my being, to give even more of myself than had yet been given. And so I'd reach and find a little more faith, a little more courage, a little more strength, and, yes, a deeper form of love. Then one day it hit me. Why should I be sad? I should be so happy for them! I should be rejoicing that they will both be free of all this pain, free of all these burdens, that they will be together again! Oh, yes! This is not a time for tears. This is a time for great joy!

And so it was that I moved out of my sorrow and back into life again, finding strength in the knowledge that life really does not end. It takes on new forms. It takes on new shapes. It reveals new vistas, but never, never ever does it end. Perhaps this was what she so much wanted me to discover for myself. Certainly it was a truth I needed to learn. Life is, and so are we!

Mother was vivid proof of that. Actually, we all are, but we take life for granted. We do not see the gift because of all the "glitter" that surrounds us, but Mother knew. In her deepest heart, she knew, and she was trying to show us. She gave us all the time we needed to get the message, for she lingered in that condition for three and a half years. Certainly much longer than any of us expected.

Such is the power of a love that is not willing to take its leave until the last deed is done. Until the last lesson has been taught. Until the final purpose has been served. And so the months, and even years, rolled by as this gentle lady in that frail little body set an example for us all.

They Are the Dreams

Where is the child who once was so carefree
Where is the youth who danced with the morn
Where is the spirit that caught the horizon
And gently carried it under her arm?

Where is the mother who sang to her baby
Where is the woman who stood so forlorn
Watering flowers that grew by the graveside
With tears that flowed from a heart so torn?

Where is the one who walked through the daisies
Who walked in the field all barefoot and free
Where is the one who greeted the sunset
And pondered just what tomorrow might be?

They are still here – No, they have not left you
They are the dance of the spirit at dawn
They are the mirrors that once did reflect you
They are the dreams that awoke with the morn.

EIGHTEEN

Getting an Answer

"Our work has to do with waking up to the largeness that is already within us."

The first sixteen months after Mother's stroke were particularly difficult. She went from crisis to crisis. It felt as though we were on a roller coaster that wouldn't stop, and I was getting to the point where I was hanging by a thread, my exhaustion was so deep.

We'd just rushed Mother over to the hospital again. She was having difficulty breathing. Finally, at 3:30 a.m., the nurses assured me she was stable so I left to go home. Just as I got to the hospital exit, I stopped and literally stamped my foot on the floor as I said, "*Something* has *got* to change!"

As soon as I said it, I realized what had to change was me. Mother wasn't doing this on purpose. She simply couldn't help what was happening with her body. The only possible thing that could change was how I responded. Suddenly I understood what is meant by the saying that it is only yourself that you experience.

It was time for me to slow down and start taking care of myself. I'd been running on fumes for quite some time being with Mother all day, every day at the nursing home, then coming home after supper and working on their home, going through everything, sorting through the accumulation of so many years, trying to get the house ready to sell. So many times my body cried out, "What about *me?*" but I couldn't stop. I not only wanted to be there for

Mother, I had promised Daddy that I would. I knew if he was here, he would just go and go and go, so that's what I did, too, but the day finally came when I had to sit down and say, "I'm sorry, Daddy, but I just can't be you anymore. I have to slow down and take care of my body."

I knew my fatigue was reaching dangerous levels, so I slowed down. Some days I only stayed with her until lunch. Occasionally I didn't go at all. Then one day I got an email telling about the Advanced Seduction of the Spirit course Deepak Chopra was offering in San Diego. Without hesitation, I signed up and left for California. Now that Mother was a little more stable, it was time for me to go and renew myself at every level.

By the time the week was over, I knew I needed to do more of this. I needed to get back to nourishing the deep levels of my being, so as new courses were offered, I went. Always I'd talk with Mother about it ahead of time, and always she encouraged me to go. And of course I shared whatever I learned with her when I got back.

Through it all, the meditation practice I'd begun in Colorado was my foundation, my anchor, no matter what I was doing. Because it made such a difference in my life, I decided to become certified so I could teach others this amazing practice. Mother supported my decision. We had talked about meditation many times. She knew it was feeding me, so I took the prerequisite courses, completed the home study course, and went out to California for the final week of on-site training.

It was a wonderful week, very intense, but so uplifting. I felt as though I was in a timeless space, doing what I was supposed to be doing. Then, about halfway through the week, it dawned on me that this was the answer to the question that had been gnawing at me ever since Neal died. This was how I could help! I could go back home and teach those children how to meditate.

I dissolved in tears at the thought. Again, the gift was so great, but the price was so dear. Even so, I came home energized and ready to move in this new direction. To my surprise, when I reached for the phone to call the mentoring foundation, there seemed to be a hand in front of my face and it seemed to be saying, "Not yet. Just wait. Be patient." This was puzzling. I really thought this was what I was supposed to do, but every time I started to make that call, there was that hand. "Okay. If you say so," was all I knew to say, and the project was put on hold.

While I was at the Chopra Center completing my certification, one of the things they suggested was that I develop a website, if I didn't already have one, so I started looking into that possibility when I got home, without success. There were people in our area who did that sort of thing, but I just wasn't able to make the right connection. Finally I just lifted it up. "If this is what You want, Lord, then You're going to have to show me how to do it." With that, I dropped the idea completely.

As you might guess, it wasn't long before I heard from Hummer. His good friend, David Max, wanted to write about Hummer on his website, www.HuskerMax.com, so Hummer gave him the article I'd written about him a couple of years earlier. Hummer said I'd probably hear from him, and he was right. David called to ask permission to use the article. He told me he doesn't pay for material he uses, but what he could do would be to link the article to my website. When I told him I didn't have a site and was having trouble finding someone to design one for me, he simply said, "Well, that's what I do." Of course. I should have known. It would all come to pass in God's own time. And it did.

The next summer I went out to Colorado to study with Jonathan Goldman once again. As we approached the gate to the ranch where he would be teaching, the air felt different somehow. I couldn't put my finger on it, but it was almost as though a "window" had opened slightly, and it puzzled me.

As the course began, the feeling became more and more intense, until by the second morning I felt rather strange and could hardly eat my breakfast. About midway through the meal, Rose, who was also attending the course, came over and put her hand on my shoulder. "Are you all right?"

"I don't know. I feel kind of dizzy, and my stomach is queasy."

"Why don't you go to your room where you can lie down. I'll come up in a few minutes and check on you."

I hadn't been in my room very long when there was a soft knock on the door. It was Rose. She came in and stood there quietly. After a moment, she came over and sat down beside me. "Donna, there's someone here. I can feel it."

"Really?"

She paused. "Yes, I think it's your husband."

"Neal?"

"Yes, he has something he wants to tell you. He wants you to know it's time now for him to move on."

"But I don't understand. I told him it was all right to go three years ago!"

"Yes, but you weren't ready then. He says you're ready now, so it's time for him to go and do the things he needs to do."

I started to cry.

"He wants you to go down to the road that leads to the ranch. There's no hurry. Whenever you feel like it." With that, she gave me a hug and left the room.

Totally overcome by this unexpected event, I just laid there, thinking about how Neal had been watching over me all this time, and I didn't even know it!

A few minutes later Monica, my roommate, came into the room. We were neighbors and had flown in together from Omaha. She started to put something away, but then she stopped and turned to me. "Donna! Someone's in the room!"

"Yes, I know."

She stood there for a moment, then almost inaudibly, "It's Neal!"

"Yes, I know."

"I don't belong here," she whispered, and she turned and left.

When I was finally able to stop crying and pull myself together, I walked down to the road.

The ranch is on a high plateau that reaches to the horizon where mountains sit in the distance. As I approached the road, I turned toward the mountains and looked across the field, not knowing what to expect.

Suddenly Neal's presence was so strong, it felt as though I could almost reach out and touch him. "Thank you, darling," I whispered. "Be well ..."

With that, the intensity of his presence became even stronger. Then slowly it began to fade away until finally he was gone. I stood there a long time gazing at the horizon, pondering the fact that Neal had waited to leave until he was sure I would be all right.

Time passed. More courses. More ideas about how I could help the kids, but always that hand appeared. I loved what I was learning and was delighted to bring back new skills, to add new facets to the teaching I now was doing. Every course, every skill found itself being woven into workshops and lectures I was giving. Even though my horizon got bigger and bigger, and the depth of my work expanded in fascinating ways, always that question haunted me.

Then one day, the thought occurred to me, *Perhaps working with these kids isn't what I'm supposed to be doing at all. I certainly don't want to be where I'm not supposed to be! Perhaps I should just forget it and move on.*

I thought about that all day, so before I climbed into bed that night, I stood by my bed and prayed, "If this isn't what You want me to do, that's okay with me. I certainly don't want to meddle. If You don't want me to do this, then neither do I, so as far as I'm concerned, I'm not going to pursue this anymore. Yes, that's right, *I quit!* If there's something You really want me to do, You're going to have to let me know in a way I can clearly understand, because until You do, I'm just going to go find something else to do—something I'd really like to do!" With that, I turned off the light and went to bed.

It was such a good feeling—such a *relief*—not to be fretting about that anymore. Now I could just get on with my life. With that happy thought, I fell into a deep sleep.

At 2 a.m. I was awakened, and there in front of me were the words:

TOOLS FOR TEENS

A COURSE IN LIFE SKILLS FOR PEOPLE ON THE GROWING EDGE

and there, beneath it, was the outline for what was to go in the course! "Oh my!" was all I could think of to say.

I did finally get back to sleep, but when I got up the next morning, I knew my work was cut out for me. It took me two weeks just to find what I needed from all the courses I'd taken. When I did, the scope of the program amazed me. I knew immediately I'd have to get permission to use all that material, so I called the Chopra Center and told them what I wanted to do. They liked the idea and asked me to send them a copy when I had it all on paper.

It took a year and a half to come up with the first full draft, and it would never have happened if my good friend Monica hadn't kept me on track. Every time I'd start to weaken and falter, she was there bolstering me up. "You have to do this, Donna! You *have* to do it!"

So I would continue, still wondering, much like Moses did, "Are you sure you have the right person, Lord?"

Monica's associate, Kathy, was so excited about the program that without my knowing it, she started contacting agencies all over the city about it. I was floored when she presented me with a notebook filled with information on the groups that were interested in the program. "But Kathy," I exclaimed, "the program isn't even half written yet!"

In spite of my occasional feelings of inadequacy, the program did come together, and it's filled with life skills for people of every age, not just teens. Throughout the course we seek to build a sense of self-worth and integrity. We show how our choices shape our life and offer skills people can practice so they can form new behavior patterns and new thought patterns, which will help them be responsible choice makers, so they can be free to explore and use their hidden talents. The course teaches healthy ways to deal with emotions, how to tap into their deep desires, and how to tune into and trust their own inner wisdom.

I was as amazed as anyone to see the depth of it. What was even more amazing was that all the time that hand had been there telling me, "Not yet. Just wait. Be patient," my prayer was being answered! I was being led to all the courses that had all the material that would ultimately go into this program!

The Chopra Center liked what they saw, and when the first copy came off the press, they sent out a notice to all their teachers. Orders came streaming in from all around the globe. People wanted to use the Tools program in venues I would never would have expected—with preschool children, in senior citizen centers, through parks and recreation departments, Veterans Administration rehab centers, Bar Mitzvah classes, youth groups, women's retreats, in prisons, and on and on.

So there I was with the program in print and orders coming in. Still not feeling totally confident, I gathered up my courage and set up an appointment with the Mid-America Council of Boy Scouts, which was the first contact on Kathy's list. When I met with the Director of Juvenile Rehabilitation, she told me they were looking for a program to use with young men who were being given a second chance by the courts. As she began listing what they wanted in the program, my eyes filled with tears. She was reciting the Table of Contents, almost verbatim.

It was at that moment I felt the program finally had come home. After all, helping these kids was what had prompted the question in the first place.

That Wild and Reckless Joy

Would that I could throw myself
Upon the altar of this life
Like the sea upon the shore
So I might know
The wild and reckless joy
That comes when all
Restraint is gone
And you've given yourself away
Utterly.

NINETEEN

Final Gifts

*"You only get one chance to live this moment,
so make it what you want it to be!"*

Mother loved the concepts in the Tools program. As the material developed, I would read portions to her and she would add bits of insight here and there. In fact, she became my sounding board. Whenever I'd get stuck, she knew just what to do, so collaborating became our secret joy. We'd formed a sort of partnership, and it was fun for both of us. Her wisdom was such a gift, her presence even more so. We just acted as though it would always be that way. Wishful thinking, I know, but I just wasn't ready yet to let go. Nor was she, so we played the game day by blessed day.

Letting go of those we love isn't easy. Instinctively we cling, but when we do, we do so out of fear. Fear sneaks up so quietly. Even when we guard our thinking, when we try to choose our feelings, circumstances can take us by surprise, and there we are—back in the same old pattern once again.

That is exactly what happened early one morning when the phone rang. So many times when someone had called, it was to say Mother was being rushed to the hospital. Off I would go again to meet them. It seemed my life was constantly being lived on the edge, and there was no relief for either of us, no matter what we did. I guess that's why I just automatically shifted into my "crisis mode" when the phone rang that particular morning.

Mother had had another stroke. They were watching her, but had not yet deemed it necessary to call the ambulance. I threw on my clothes, flew out the door with a piece of toast in my hand, and headed down the highway. I wasn't speeding, but I was going the limit when a car passed me. When I saw what the license plate said—U R OK—I could hardly believe my eyes.

"Of course!" I thought to myself. "I'm okay, and Mother is okay, and this is just part of the journey!" Immediately I was filled with an indescribable sense of peace. My adrenaline level started going down, and by the time I reached the nursing home, I was absolutely calm. Every last trace of fear was gone, leaving only this profound sense of peace.

When I walked into Mother's room, she was glad to see me, but she was frightened. She didn't understand what was happening, and she didn't feel well. I sat down beside her and lovingly held her hand. I could feel the peace enfolding both of us. As it did, she began to settle down, so we spent the day just talking and reminiscing and sharing our love.

When someone is so very ill, you wouldn't think it would be possible to have a good day, but that's exactly what happened. There, surrounded by that ineffable peace, we had one of the most beautiful days together we'd ever had.

Someone told me once, "If you knew Who walks beside you, you'd never be afraid again." For a long time I wasn't sure what that meant. Now I knew, and it made all the difference. Life isn't about fear at all. It's about love, a love that flows from some deep, hidden stream. When we drink from that stream, nothing is ever the same again.

And so the days and weeks continued. During the three and a half years that followed Mother's first stroke, I helped her in every way I could. This was as it should be, as it needed to be, and I knew that. But I also was keenly aware that in her own way, Mother was offering me lessons I had no other way to learn. Difficult as it was for both of us, I will always be grateful for the time we had together.

Mother encouraged me in my studies. She loved hearing about the courses I was taking and found a special kind of joy in our "deep discussions" as we explored our spiritual horizons together. I have no doubt that she could see I was building some sort of meaning and purpose for my life. Little did I know that I was also moving toward the time when she would know it was all right to leave us, to go and be with Daddy. Perhaps that was my gift to her, working toward the time where she could be at peace about saying that final goodbye.

It was after one of our discussions that she looked at me and said, "You're making a life for yourself, aren't you?"

The question surprised me, so I said the only thing I could think of to say. "I've had to, Mother. It was either that or sit here and cry the rest of my life, and I didn't think you'd want me to do that." She just nodded her head, but I could see she was thinking.

From that point forward, Mother's condition began to fail. She knew I was going to be all right, so now she could let go and move on. I didn't understand that at the time, but in looking back, I could see that was indeed what was happening.

The changes that occurred in Mother's priorities after her stroke reminded us all of what is really important in life. All the busy things she usually filled her life with just fell away, allowing her beautiful, gracious spirit to shine through. It was almost as though we could see into her soul.

Mother had a stalwart spirit. Even though she had been robbed of all ability to care for herself, she taught us so much during this period of her life—like how to accept the worst sort of calamity with grace, how to put up with all the indignities that not being able to care for yourself entailed, and how to minister to others in spite of all of the above. Even though her body failed her, her spirit was a light to everyone around her. She showed us all that what you are is so much more important than what you do. She could "do" so very little, but she didn't need to. What she was, was more than adequate.

If ever I received a lesson in acceptance—*total* acceptance—it was from my mother. She simply did not complain. More than that, she spent her days making sure everyone around her knew how very special, how very beautiful, they were. Her presence was like a magnet, attracting people from all over the building. They'd stop by to see how she was. Did she need something? How was she today? And they always left feeling better because they had come. Because they had cared.

This proved to be a crucial part of Mother's legacy at the nursing home, because both men and women from varied ethnic backgrounds worked on her hall. That meant men would be helping her with some of her personal needs. Having to accept help from a man of any color stretched her to her limit. Eventually she conquered even that.

I didn't realize the extent of that victory until two days after her passing. I was at the nursing home packing up her things when I happened across Billie, one of the young black men who was on duty. Since "Billie" had been Mother's nickname during her younger years, Billie and Mother had formed a special bond. Billie had just learned about Mother's passing, and he was thoroughly shaken. Throwing his arms around me, he stood there and wept. "We loved her, you know," was all he could finally say, and of course, I did know. It was obvious just by the tender way he had cared for her. It was a two-way street, if ever there was one.

One of Mother's final gifts had to do with fear itself. When the final stages of congestive heart failure began in earnest, fear gripped my heart. What was going on, and why was I responding like this? I thought I'd moved beyond fear, but apparently not.

"Fight or flight" was the answer a good friend gave me. Of course! But if that is so, then I have a choice! That's when I remembered the lesson from many weeks ago: this isn't about fear at all, it's about love! Little did I know the important role that realization would play in later days.

So instead of filling our remaining time together with fear, we just slipped a little deeper into a love that seemed to be flowing from that deep, hidden stream, a love that assured us both that regardless of what was happening to Mother's physical body, she was all right. This was just part of her journey.

I began to understand in a new sort of way that there really is no death. There is only life. True, we leave our body behind us, but *we* go on. *We* do not die. That is why life is so wonderful. It changes, but it does not end!

Once I understood this—really understood it—the trauma just slipped away, replaced by an indescribable sense of wonder. It was that wonder, that peace, which allowed me to be present to her in a way that reached beyond my own ability to respond. This was about a love beyond definition, a love that carries us through even the most difficult events.

Weeks later, when that final phone call came, we rode through her last day on wings that bore us up and allowed us to enter into what can only be described as a sacred space in which love and beauty were the only reality for both of us.

It seems strange now to be looking back at all this. In many ways this period of her life seemed so long, but now it seems like it was just an instant, a blink of the eye. Many were the times I tried to understand why Mother was still here, why she continued to put up with all that she endured. Part of it, I believe, was that it's just so hard to say goodbye to your family, and Mother loved her family very much.

Another key to the puzzle, at least as I see it, was that she was challenging me to tap the deep resources of my being. She needed to know I would be able to manage after she was gone. She truly was a mother to the very end.

Mother's passing was different from my two previous losses. Both my husband and my father were snatched away so suddenly. Not so with Mother. Hers was a graceful passage. We'd had the whole day together, and while she hadn't been able to say a word, words hadn't been necessary. We seemed to be enveloped in a sacred space, and we were content just to be there, to let happen what was happening. Knowing that neither of us could stop it, we were able to accept it for what it was, as she slipped into the sacred mystery we have yet to fathom.

As I said at her service, Mother lived a gracious life, and she died a gracious death. Sudden passages can be such a shock. For me, they have triggered buckets and buckets of tears, but with Mother it was different, and that was the biggest surprise of all.

Oh, yes, I've cried, but that night, after I finally returned home and got ready for bed, I found myself smiling. I was just so happy for them, and I knew they knew it. I could almost see them there in the room with me, smiling and happy and radiant. So we laughed together, and we smiled, and at one point I thought I heard them saying, "Well, we did it, didn't we!"

"Yes, we did," I answered, "and it was good—*very* good!"

My Pure Repast

Do not weep for me, my child,
For I am free at last
Of all of the encumbrances
That held me in their grasp.
Now my spirit freely soars,
Released from all its pain,
And heights I could not reach before
Now hold no stress or strain.
Transcendent joy is mine at last,
Immortal Love my pure repast,
So do not grieve, do not despair –
Look in your heart—I will be there.

TWENTY

The Larger View

"One of your deepest truths has to do with Who You Are."

After having watched the serenity with which Mother made her passing, I found myself wondering how I would handle my own death when that time came. Would I be able to go peacefully, like Mother did? What thoughts would I have? What approach would I take?

Certainly letting go—not just of personal possessions but of personal relationships—would have to be part of that. I know at some point we have to let go, willing or not, but how would I do that? Would I be able to reach beyond all that's out here and move peacefully into that other space that has always been our home? And if I could, would I do it willingly? Even joyfully?

That seemed like a lot to ask. Perhaps it was too soon for me to reach that far, but I knew I was going to have to come to grips with this one way or another before I could get on with my life.

Since I was needing answers, I started reading about answers others have found, and I learned there are a lot of ways to look at death. Cultures in other parts of the world say death is just an illusion. They believe that when the soul has reached its maximum level for evolution in a physical body, it sheds that body, much like a caterpillar does. The life force that expresses itself as the caterpillar does not die, and neither does the soul.

If they are right, then perhaps we need a fresh lens through which to view the question. Perhaps death just means a change in awareness. If it is only the body that dies, if the soul truly does go on, then what is it that we fear? Is it the unknown we are uncomfortable with? Is it separation from those we love? As human beings, fear of the unknown runs deep. Certainly the greatest unknown for most of us is death.

Change, especially significant change, is not easy to embrace. Neither is separation, but can we really be separated? Perhaps separation is an illusion, too. Yes, we experience separation at the physical level, but at the level of spirit, at the level of our soul, aren't we still connected? If we are all "cut out of the same cloth," if we really are formed from the same substance, then how can we be separated?

Some of my children live almost 2,000 miles from me, but still we are very close. We do not get to see each other very often, but we are "together" in our hearts every day. Would this be any less so just because someone is no longer "in the body"? True, we cannot see our loved ones who have gone on before us, but the love is still there. Because our love connects us, I do not feel separated from my children. Why, then, would I feel separated from those who are no longer here?

Love does not die. There are those who say that ultimately we do not die either, even though we do leave the body. Surely this should be cause for hope—and, yes, for joy—even in the midst of our grief.

Part of the problem, at least as I see it, is our tendency to seek security in what we can touch. We are reluctant to let go, fearful we might lose that on which we have based our stability, yet whatever we can touch must ultimately change. That is why letting go just might be part of the answer. Letting go bestows freedom and breaks the bonds of the fear that entraps us. Letting go opens our eyes to the truth that nothing is ever really lost.

Perhaps if we lived knowing we have one foot here and one foot in eternity, the transition would be easier to accept. We simply are not this mortal body. We use it for a while, but when the body cannot serve us any longer, "we" are still intact.

Ancient Eastern sages not only embraced this concept, they found it brought clarity and meaning to their earthly existence. Because they understood we are flesh and blood and spirit at the same time, they were able to see death as a moment of great change, even of great awakening. Ancient scriptures tell us death rends the veil of our misunderstanding and allows us to see how we are part of one great, indivisible whole. Tibetan sages call that whole "the infinite expanse." They say to catch even a glimpse of that pure expanse is to behold the source of all that is manifest.

The sages found it helpful to compare that expanse to the ocean. They said we are like individual waves that emerge on its surface. When the energy behind the wave is spent, it returns to its source. The same is true for us. That return for rest and renewal is what we call death.

Death, then, can be seen as a time of release, a time of liberation from the limitations that have bound us. That time of transition is also said to be a moment of great joy because it restores the memory of who we really are. In that remembering we see the great cosmic dance and begin to understand our part in its infinite display.

The ancients aren't the only ones who viewed death in this way. Christianity assures us there is indeed life after death. In fact, it promises eternal life. If this is so, then surely it is only where we are that changes.

Near-death experiences and death-related visions testify to this as well. Those who have had such encounters tell us we are not human beings hoping for a spiritual experience; we are spiritual beings who are having a human experience.

Deep down in our heart, I think most of us already know we are souls in disguise. The problem is, the roles we are playing feel so real, we think they are our only reality. Because this reality does not satisfy our deep inner longing, eventually our search for meaning and purpose—and love—turns inward.

When I was about four years old, I remember standing in our front yard surveying my surroundings and knowing somehow that I had been here before. It was as though a door behind me hadn't quite closed as yet. I couldn't see where the door went, but I knew I had come through it. As clearly as though it was yesterday, I remember looking around, sighing a little, and saying, "Well, here I go again. I sure hope I get it right this time!"

Just what was it I needed to get right? I've pondered that question all my life. While I still don't have the answer, that experience left me with a certainty that this was not my first visit to this planet.

No doubt you have had moments just as profound. What do such events say to us? Is this a school we are in? If so, what are we here to learn? Are we preparing for work we are yet to do when we leave here? Are we learning to tune in to that larger reality of which we are a part? Where is the path that leads to it? How do we learn to heed its call, to glimpse the view of which the ancients spoke?

Joan Halifax says the inner call is more often felt than heard. She believes we hear that call more clearly as we learn to care about each other. In reaching out, in lifting up, we quicken the gentle side of our nature. In learning to be more sensitive to the needs of others, we open the way to a deeper form of love.

In The Path to Love, Deepak Chopra encourages us to come from love every moment we can because love is what life is all about. Deepak goes on to say that every lesson, no matter what it is, is really about love, that all the ups and downs of life really do work together toward love's purpose.

And what is that purpose? We find at least part of our answer when we reach out to others. In nurturing others, we nurture ourselves. In loving others, we heal ourselves. As our compassion broadens and deepens our awareness of our shared spirituality, gradually we glimpse that larger view, that infinite expanse within which we are all contained. From this truer perspective we begin to see ourselves more as the ocean and less as individual waves. Our feeling of oneness erases our sense of separation and restores a feeling of wholeness that defies even death.

Ancient and modern sages have found this to be true. As for me, I have to admit I probably won't know during this lifetime if I "got it right," but I do have a sense that, mistakes and all, I'm closer than I was. I think that may be how it is for most of us.

We fear death because we fear change, but life is not about fear. Life is about love. Life is only about love. When we know that— truly know that—everything changes. We see through a different window. We come from a different perspective, and we respond from a deeper level, a level that knows only love.

How do we find that wholeness? How do we find that love? There is no compass to follow, other than what is in our heart, but if we let our heart lead us, eventually we will discover a growing sense of harmony and peace, and yes, of being on the path that leads to the wholeness we are seeking.

Perhaps this is why the ancient sages placed so much importance on the art of living well and dying well. They saw all the nuances of living and dying as threads in a tapestry of divine design, weaving together a pattern that would ultimately reveal what our Creator had in mind all along. That is why their message is just as relevant today as it was then: When we make peace with our death, we begin to make peace with our life also. In that peace, our view expands beyond the finite to that "infinite expanse," which is our eternal home.

Passing Through

Death is but a broadening of sight,
A moving out of darkness into light,
And as your essence thus becomes refined
So also do you move into the heart of mind.
It is a moment, then, of sweet release
Imbued with such transcending peace
That were it seen like this before
The soul would welcome such a door
And gently pass its being through
Into the realm of life anew.

TWENTY ONE

The Call and the Challenge

"Your horizons are really within you."

S o much had happened in just seven years, it would have been easy to remain in my grief after Mother was gone. Far easier to stay with a sinking ship and go valiantly down with it than to begin again, to face the new, the unknown, but I knew I could not do that, not if I wanted to honor the gift of life I was still being given.

Of course, making that decision is not the same as acting on it. The "wide open spaces" can be pretty intimidating when you aren't accustomed to going it alone, and I must admit that right then I was feeling very much alone. It was a whole new frontier out there. To enter it meant *decisions*. It meant *choices*. It meant stopping and getting re-acquainted with myself after all these many years.

As I thought about it, I could see I had become so caught up in living my life that I didn't know who I really was. And yet, if I didn't know that, how could I ever hope to explore the inner landscape of my soul? How could I hope to discover the meaningful pursuits that have been waiting to unfold at precisely this very time in my life? How could I ever find out what I am capable of becoming when I don't even know what I am?

This dilemma is not uncommon in times of transition. It takes courage to let go of the past. Letting go is a commitment you make to yourself to go forward, to live in the Now, to explore the unknown, to search for the treasures hidden deep within yourself, which you have yet to access and employ. Not to do so would be the greatest tragedy of all, for are we not all here to bring the very best we have to life? To explore our potential? To use our gifts in the service of others? All this, and more, becomes possible when we are willing to let go of the past and move into the present, when we are willing to go inside ourselves—deep inside ourselves—and find what we have been looking for all along.

To do so is to enter an exciting time, a time when you discover things about yourself you never knew. A time when you remember what you had forgotten long ago. It's a time to blossom, a time to grow, a time to unfold. It's a time to discover inner joys that nourish and enrich the soul, that bring a quality and a depth to your daily living, which cannot help but enhance all that you do. It's a time for peace, a time for love. As you press on in these new waters, the unexpected graces your life, opening channels you have not yet dreamed of, ways to go you have not even thought of, opportunities to bring even more of yourself to life.

It is the beginning really, the beginning of be-ing, of *really* be-ing perhaps for the very first time, of living with yourself, of getting to know yourself, cherishing and nourishing the Self that has been so faithful in all you have come through thus far. And, yes, giving that Self a chance to do what it has been waiting to do for so long—to teach you what you have always wanted to know about life, and about Who You Are.

After the pain, after the heartache, after all the struggle, after the freeing and letting go, then comes the wholeness, even the One-ness as you return to your center where you are safe and secure, where you most truly are yourself. Thus out of your own heart's gift do you receive a blessing that nothing—not even death—can take away. In giving the gift of freedom, so do you receive that same gift yourself. With that gift comes a joy that even sorrow cannot defeat.

This, then, is both the call and the challenge. If you are among the valiant few who have chosen to heed the call, I salute you. Know that your guide is within you. The path awaits. It is time to go within, to explore new lands and do things you've never done before. Truly, it will be a journey unlike all others, but you need not fear, for now, at last, you will come to know yourself. You will find out you are grander than you ever knew, and when you do, the deep longing in your heart will be filled.

Would You?

What is this love
You say you are seeking?
Do you want it enough
To climb the high mountains?
Would you endure the
Cracked and parched lips
Of desert lands?
How great is the longing
You say you have
Inside you?
If the price were
All of this
Would you render it
Gladly
To taste one sweet moment
Of bliss?

TWENTY TWO

A Lesson in Humility

"Love is constantly seeking to spread its wings through us."

If someone were to ask me if the learning process ever ends, I think I'd have to say, "No." At least that's how it has been for me.

First you grasp a concept, then life gives you the opportunity to integrate your new knowledge into how you live your life. Then you're given another concept to work on as you continually broaden your horizons and explore your hidden potential. That potential would never be tapped were you not forced to go within yourself to find that inner strength, to mine that inner beauty, to tap those depths of wisdom that reside at the core of your being.

One does not refine metal without burning away the dross. One does not end up with gold without having first gone through the fire. Even such common things as iron are strengthened by repeatedly being thrust into the cauldron, creating a durable inner core in the process.

That is what life does, I think. If we can know that, it becomes so much easier to work with the process. Then, when the tough times come, and we know they will, if we can see them as opportunities to shore up our spirit and strengthen our soul, they, too, can become our friend, for surely the day will come when we will look back on where we have been and see what life has taught us. We will see how it has brought us to where we are.

Yes, life can be difficult, but if it wasn't, what reason would we have to strive and grow? What would motivate us to reach for the heights? It would be so easy to just float along, to bask on the beach of life, and never encounter those great waves that force us to use all our resources just to keep afloat.

Gratefully, we are not always in the thick of battle, but there must be battles if we are ever to become victors in the game of life. Always, our battles are first won in our heart. It happens inside us before it can happen anywhere else, and when it has happened in your heart, it *has* happened.

Since it felt like I'd been doing a lot of that, I was especially grateful for the opportunity to just stop and reflect after Mother was gone. I gave myself the time I needed to look back, to assess how I had handled things, to see where I was weak and where I was strong. Things I could have done differently came clearly to the front of my mind. Of course, the subject of death was always there. I wanted to honor Mother and Daddy and Neal not only by the way I lived the rest of my life but by how I met death as well. It was an awesome task, but I knew I had to find a way to do it. The pieces were all there. It was just a matter of figuring it out.

I'd been pondering things like this for several months after Mother died when one day my phone rang. It was Mae, who was both neighbor and close friend to Neal's cousin. "Have you seen Margaret lately?"

"No, I've talked with her, but I haven't seen her. Why do you ask?"

"I think you need to see her. She's having problems."

"What kind of problems, Mae?"

"I keep finding her wandering in the hall, lost and not knowing where she is. Other times she'll be sitting in her apartment feeling frightened and confused. She's losing ground, if you ask me."

"I'll be right over."

What I found wasn't pretty. Margaret was confused and feeling very insecure, which was a total turn-around for her. Having worked for a local podiatrist into her early eighties, she had been the picture of clarity and good health, but not now. The first thing she said when she saw me was, "You're in charge. I can't do it anymore."

Mae and Margaret had been looking at an independent living facility not far away, so we made an appointment to visit it. We liked what we saw and thought perhaps not having to cook or drive would take care of the problem, so we signed a contract.

Since I was Margaret's trustee, it was up to me to begin the process of going through all her things, helping her decide what to keep and what to give away. I couldn't believe this was happening all over again. It seemed like just yesterday I'd finished doing all that for Mother and Daddy. Now here I was, doing it for Margaret, too. It was an enormous task, and all the confusion it created just made Margaret's condition worse.

Moving day was a nightmare. I'd accepted the offer of friends to move her, thinking they would do it all. I'd worn myself out with all the packing and decision making, so was looking forward to being able to sit back and watch. It never happened. There I was, carrying boxes, loading trucks, right along with everyone else.

When we finally got to the new location, we parked Margaret in a chair in her new apartment and told her to stay right there while we went downstairs for more boxes. We weren't gone even five minutes, but when we got back she was nowhere in sight. We searched everywhere and couldn't find her. Finally I went over to the office to see about another key, and there she was, coming down the hall, a full block and a half away from her apartment, with no idea how she got there.

People took turns staying with her the first few nights to help her get oriented, but it was clear she was going to need more help than that place offered, so I started visiting assisted living facilities in our area. I don't know about where you live, but we have a lot of them in our area, and I visited them all. Finally, the last one, the Marquis Place, answered her needs.

Again, the decisions, the downsizing, the packing, the moving. This time I hired a moving company, but that, too, was a disaster. They didn't bring boxes, and they didn't expect to do the packing, even though that had been our agreement on the phone. By the time we got her moved and unpacked, I was so exhausted I was shaking, so I went home and went to bed.

At six the next morning, the phone rang. "Margaret has fallen and dislocated her hip. We've called the ambulance. Can you meet them at the hospital?" This time I had to say, "No." I knew if I went, I'd end up in the hospital, too. I was just that depleted. I called my sister-in-law, Louise, who spent the next twelve hours at the hospital seeing Margaret through surgery and getting her settled back into her room.

After several days, Margaret was back at the Marquis, set up for the rehab she needed. I breathed a sigh of relief. Perhaps now things would settle down, but it was not to be. Four weeks later, I got another call. She'd dislocated her hip—again. This time there was no choice in the matter. The level of care she now required made it necessary for her to go directly to a nursing home from the hospital. Fortunately, after a bit of scrambling, I was able to get her into the same one where Mother had been.

Of course, that meant I had the packing to do all over again. This time I just packed it all up to store in my garage. I'd sort through it later. It was almost Christmas and I was worn out. Whatever energy I'd had left after losing Mother had been spent on Margaret, and then some.

The many trips back and forth began again. By the time I got the last box closed at the Marquis, I was trembling. *I could sure use two strong young men right about now,* I thought to myself. When I looked up, two strong young men were standing in the door, complete with Santa hats, broad smiles, and packages in their hands! For a moment I thought they were angels, the answer to my prayer had come so quickly. Later I learned they were actually the sons of her investment broker.

"Margaret?" they asked.

"No," so I told them what had happened and where she was. They were about to leave and go to the nursing home, when I added, "But I could surely use some help getting all this loaded into my car."

No sooner said than done. They were happy to help, and I couldn't have been more grateful. After my good friend Ginny met me at my house and unloaded the car for me, I went inside and went to bed. *I'm not getting up until I feel like it*, I told myself, and that's just what I did. I slept around the clock for two days. It was a good thing I did, because Margaret was on a roller coaster, in and out of the hospital, just as Mother had been, for six months before things finally leveled off.

As the weeks went by, I couldn't help wondering why I was doing this *again*. While I was deeply sympathetic to Margaret's situation, I had a feeling that her care had fallen in my lap because there was still more to learn. I started thinking about what Jesus meant when he said, "Inasmuch as you have done it unto one of the least of these, you have done it unto me" (Matthew 25:40).

That thought tied in so well with what I'd been reading about how we are all one, how the divine presence is here, in everything and everyone. I tried to imagine how being connected like that would work. What would it feel like? What would it mean? How would it change the way I saw things, the way I did things? I had a sense of it, but instinctively I knew there was more—far more—to it than I had yet glimpsed.

After about a year and a half, things settled down to the extent that Margaret could enter into some of the activities at the nursing home. Then, in the spring of the following year, she seemed even stronger, so I decided to try to get her to her church. Since she was confined to a wheelchair, I arranged for a local transport company to get us there and back. Margaret was thrilled. As her old friends welcomed her with genuine warmth, I stood there and watched a transformation take place. She acted so bright and cheerful, even affirming how well she was, almost like her old self again.

Since our adventure went so well, I started thinking about trying to get her to church during the Christmas season later that year. As the time approached, we both were excited at the prospect of going again, of seeing her old friends and enjoying the music and festivities. To our surprise, a fifty-piece orchestra was setting up the morning we went. *How nice!* I thought, as they tuned their instruments in preparation for the service, not realizing what lay in store.

Suddenly the sanctuary was filled with such glorious music, it literally took my breath away. It was as though the gates of heaven had opened and the music came streaming into our hearts. I'd never experienced anything like it. Immediately my eyes filled with tears at the sacredness of the moment. Everything was holy. The church was holy. The music was holy. And Margaret, poor, dear Margaret in her broken body, was holy. I was flooded with humility and gratitude and felt so honored that I could be there, doing that with her. It was all I could do to keep from weeping openly over the beauty of the gift we were being given. Probably for the first time in my life I understood what humility is really all about.

"School" was definitely still in session.

I Should Have Known, Lord

Was that You, Lord?
Was it You my soul was seeking?
Was it You Who touched me in the dark
When I was barely sleeping?

And all the many tears I shed,
When all my being cried,
Are You the One Who came and stood
So gently by my side?

Oh Lord, there were so many times
When, groping in the night,
I felt a hand reach out to me
To take away my fright,

And as the weeks would slip away
That Presence grew and grew.
Oh yes, I should have known, Lord,
That always it was You!

TWENTY THREE

Taking a Quantum Leap

"When you find yourself, you open the door to the Infinite."

Gradually things settled into a more balanced rhythm, and I was able to get back to the business of living my life while still tending to Margaret's needs. I attended more of Deepak's courses, became certified to teach yoga, and continued studying with Jonathan Goldman, all the while wondering, *What more can I learn from this? What is life trying to teach me?*

Along the way, Deepak introduced us to Dr. David Morehouse and Remote Viewing, so I studied with David, too. I'd heard of Remote Viewing before but never really understood how it worked. It was fascinating.

The principle behind Remote Viewing is that everything, at its basic level, is energy. That energy is conscious, and it is intelligent. We exist in a field of energy that science is now recognizing as the unified field because *everything* is energy! This means we are part of that field. We are conscious energy (spirit) expressing on a physical plane.

Remote Viewing, as David calls it, teaches us to direct our attention to the conscious energy field so we can explore that field. All sentient beings are expressions of this universal intelligence, this conscious, divine matrix that is expressing itself through myriad forms and phenomena. Once we recognize that we are part of that matrix, we can then move consciously into the unified field and be anywhere, at any point in time. This is possible because spirit is boundless. Spirit is everywhere, and we are spirit. This means that our spiritual or universal nature is everywhere, too!

This is true for all of us. We all have the capacity to tap into levels beyond what the physical senses define and move into areas that reach beyond the borders of the mind. We all have the capacity to learn this. As we do this, and then integrate this new knowledge into our experience, we consciously become what we know.

This may seem like a lot to grasp if you've not thought about it before. We're so accustomed to limiting our perception of ourselves to a physical body that perceives with a mind, but we are so much more than that. Traditionally, as human beings, our attention is focused on the material aspect of our nature. Once we realize that we are spiritual beings expressing through a physical form, we can begin directing our attention to our spiritual nature, too, and from there into its universality, because as spirit, we are boundless, unlimited, and eternal.

This, then, is what David was teaching us to do. He led us through sessions that included practice searches outward into the manifest field, both on and off this planet. It was amazing to see how the mind's eye could see these things, not perfectly, but still with such detail as to know we had actually accessed that site. The beauty of this practice is that when you have many people working on the same target, or the same site, as it is called, the composite of that information gives you sufficient knowledge to have a good idea of what you are looking at.

This practice isn't limited just to the here and now. You can also look into the future, as well as the past, and more importantly, at least from my point of view, is that you can go deep within yourself and access your own inner wisdom. You can ask questions and receive amazing answers. You can seek guidance and find clarity. This training was the perfect lead-in for what was about to happen when I attended Deepak's new course, *Secrets of Enlightenment.*

One of the things Deepak frequently talks about during his courses is the phenomenon known as a quantum leap, whereby a jump or a shift from one place to another occurs without there being any intervening space or time. In other words, one moment you are here, and the next moment you are there. Without my knowing it, I was about to make my own quantum leap. That leap proved to be the high point of all my studies thus far.

Toward the end of Deepak's course, his partner, Dr. David Simon, led us through a profound meditation that gradually took me beyond my present lifetime, then beyond this universe, then even beyond all space and time into the very heart of that Sacred Center where there is no thought, no language, no sense of "I, me, or mine," only Pure Being. Pure Awareness. Light beyond description. Love beyond measure. Unending, unutterable Silence. Ineffable, eternal Is-ness, unfolding and expressing Itself again and again as the Infinite I Am. I wish I could tell you what it was like being there, being That, but there just aren't words.

I don't know how long I was there, but when I began moving back toward time and space, in my heart I knew, "That's what I am ... and That's what you are ... and That's what all this is ... and That's really all there is!" This is what the ancient sages have been trying to tell us. Now I know why.

One never knows when that elusive window will open and suddenly, without even knowing what is about to happen, there you are. More than you could have imagined, far more than you would have even hoped for, the realization dawns. All that you had thought was true, all you believed was real simply falls away, leaving you with only one thing—an unshakable understanding for which there is no language. The gift is beyond being profound. It is the Truth you have longed to remember all these many and varied lives. Now that it is here, you witness it in awe, knowing there is nothing else you can do.

Suffice it to say that holy encounter answered all my questions. Of course, as so often happens, it also left me with new questions just as deep and just as profound, such as how do I re-orient myself in this time-space experience with this new knowledge? How do I live here—now—in light of this new understanding? I could see that part of the task before me was to take what I had gained back to my daily life and incorporate what I had inwardly come to know.

After such an unforgettable experience, coming back to "ordinary daily life" became somewhat of a puzzle. Everything seemed so trivial, so mundane. What could possibly be the purpose of all this, and why are we squandering lifetimes in such meaningless pursuits? Perhaps it is through such pursuits that we must learn to find the indescribable. Certainly, *That Which Is* is undeniably hidden in all things. To understand that is one thing. To see it is another.

I can only guess the difference it would make if we could all do this. To see everything as sacred, and respond accordingly, would transform this world so we might never recognize it as having come from what it presently seems to be.

If this be so, then our work is certainly cut out for us. At least it is for me. Seeing through the veil, not just in illumined moments, but all the time would have to require such focus, such dedication that all else must fall by the wayside, and yet, what else could matter quite as much? To walk consciously in the presence of the One That Is makes any price seem small. To say it is a discipline would not quite be true, for while it most certainly would require discipline, it would be more a labor of love, a pursuit of the extraordinary, and ultimately a conscious blending of all the parts into one undeniable Whole.

I think you could safely say life's lessons are about learning to see, and, yes, learning to be—to be what we are already, whether we are conscious of it or not. Now, having been there, having seen That, the indelible memory is the only thing worth desiring, worth following. While we must still continue our earthly labors, they have been put into a different framework somehow. Knowing what we now know to be true, nothing will ever be the same again.

Always before when I completed a class, I left wanting more and more and more. This time I came away so filled that all I wanted to do was give back. So again, the questions, How can I serve? How can I help? were at the front of my mind. There were other questions, too. Big questions, such as, How do I apply this broader understanding to my everyday life? How do I integrate this new knowledge? How does what I now know fit into this picture? And where do I go from here? Fortunately, help was on the way.

David Morehouse's training is done in five levels. I had completed three of them and had scheduled the final two levels for the fall of that same year. It proved to be a good decision, because it was at David's course that some of my answers appeared. In David's unique way, he strengthened our ability to move consciously into the unified field so we could experience the universal aspect of our nature.

My perception of the world was definitely shifting. I was no longer seeing things as "good" or "bad." Things just are. The key, then, is to do as Jon Kabat-Zinn suggests and learn to ride the surf, instead of being pulled under by it. In other words, learn to recognize the rhythm of life's events as they fluctuate between times of learning and times of rest and preparation. We have periods of intense learning (if we are willing), and times of what I like to think of as cocooning, which is just naturally followed by periods of emergence into new growth patterns that our learning created.

Toward the end of the fourth level of our training, David led us through an open search inward. There were questions we were to address, the most basic of which, for me at least, were, Where do I go from here? What do you want me to do next?

I moved through all the protocols as I prepared myself to receive answers to these questions, but there was nothing, only silence. I sensed I needed to go more deeply, that I had to let go of all expectations. I was at the point where I could feel myself bringing closure to some of the things in my life. I knew I was preparing for something new, even though I didn't know yet what that would be, but I had to be willing to let go completely. That is what I tried to do there in the silence as I surrendered more and more to the higher wisdom.

Still, no answer. Then, just as the session was coming to a close, I heard the words, "You have a story to tell." Immediately I knew what it was referring to, and it brought tears of recognition to my eyes. I had begun this manuscript after Neal died, but now there was so much more to say. So much more light had come upon my path. It was indeed time to finish the book. It was time to tell people how those events that were so difficult proved to be such great blessings. In looking back, I do remember the pain, the grief, the struggle, but now I also see the great gift that they were.

Truly, life is a paradox. For me, the paradox has been one of having lived in both light and shadow, always seeking the light, but not always being able to find it consciously. Although I have always been aware of a guiding influence, the choices were mine as to whether I followed that guidance.

Even so, whether I did or not, always I was being drawn toward the light. Always I was learning, growing, and unfolding as I moved from one plateau to another, walking through valleys but ever pressing forward in the conviction that nothing is ever wasted if I could just hang on and let things unfold as they were supposed to.

My mental, emotional, physical, and spiritual well-being has been an unfaltering mirror of how well I was attuned to my own true nature. As I became more aligned with that nature, joy came into my life. I'm not talking about the "happiness" you might find in getting something or doing something. I'm talking about the joy that can only happen within you, the joy that is not dependent on anything outside you, the joy of simply being.

When I found my own inner silence, I found the peace and light and joy that have always been within me. Thus I moved from learning to becoming, and from becoming to being. The shift was gradual, like the unfolding of a rose. At my own speed, in my own way, an inner presence was revealed of which I simply had not conceived ahead of time, even though I was being drawn toward it as though by some invisible, irresistible magnet.

So how does one learn to hear that inner call? Since it comes from the silence, you might begin by paying attention to the silence, wherever you are. In fact, do it right now. Just stop reading this and listen to the silence. No thought. No activity. Just be still, and listen.

If you are really listening, you will probably become aware of a listener. That listener is you. It is your eternal presence. That eternal presence is your soul, and it is always there. When you can carry the awareness of your soul with you, your awareness deepens, and you begin to experience the silence where words are no longer needed. You just Are, and that is more than enough.

So more and more now, let the space around you be the Presence. Let the silence be the Sound. Let your movement be a stirring from the Source within you. Let your mind be quiet so as not to miss the inner leading from moment to moment. Then your activity can be a spilling out from the spirit within, for life is a flow—a flow of energy, a flow of love. You are part of the grand design that moves the clouds and illumines the stars. So, too, will you be illumined by the light that shines in your silence, the love that pours through your heart, the life that courses through you, quickening and enlivening you in every way, for you are that light. That is what you have been, what you are, and what you are becoming.

There is always so much more than you have yet imagined, so trust the process. Know that all things are working toward some good purpose, whether you can see it or not. Learn to live with equanimity, accepting what happens with grace and peace. Rather than labeling things as good or bad, look for the lesson within them. Watch for what life is trying to teach you. Go with the flow and enjoy the journey.

Life is a continuum, so celebrate your life! Celebrate the beauty of it and the gifts it brings so lavishly when you are open to them. Live your life with joy and gratitude. Meet each day with eagerness to press on, and most of all, seek to become the love that has supported and sustained you through all of this. In that love is the wholeness you have been seeking.

To my thinking, this would be enough—more than enough—to fill our lives with beauty and with grace.

By What Grace

Who is it that wanders thus
Through flower-strewn fields
And star-lit skies?
What silent majesty doth stand
In ageless peaks
Where grandeur hides
In towering trees
That watch the ages
Come and go?
Whose mighty power
Imbues the seas
With universes yet unknown
By mortal man?
By what grace does intellect
Allow the soul to ponder thus,
Or love to soar
And soaring, free
The sacred soul
From mortal dust?

TWENTY FOUR

A Door Opens Wide

*"Life knows what we're supposed
to be doing, even when we don't."*

One of the things having a broader perspective teaches you is to be flexible, to go with the flow, and to welcome the unexpected into your life. As long as you're mentally locked into expectations, you limit what can come your way. Once you learn to let the universe lead the way, amazing things begin to happen. That's why asking open-ended questions, such as "How can I help? How can I serve?" is so powerful. It opens you to a higher plan, something you yourself can't imagine or orchestrate, but that will come through you if you are receptive. That is exactly what started to happen with me.

I was well into the writing of this book when I received an invitation to an open house at Uta Halee/Cooper Village, two residential treatment centers for boys and girls who have had a really tough start in life. I remembered hearing Mother talk about these centers when I was a child but had never seen them, so I decided to go.

That is where I met Tracy Wells, the Director of Donor Relations. We hit it off right away and decided to meet for lunch sometime soon. As a result of that lunch, I was invited to start teaching meditation to the young residents at these centers. What a privilege that proved to be! The kids were so receptive. It was beautiful.

I'd been doing that for a while when I got an email from Hummer, telling me about a friend he'd met at a Raiders camp thirty years ago who was now coaching at-risk kids in Sacramento. Because the need was so great, his friend started Playmakers Mentoring Foundation to better serve the kids he was coaching.

Playmakers was having their first fund raiser and his friend wanted Hummer to speak, but Hummer doesn't travel anymore, so he agreed to write a letter, knowing I'd "help him with the commas." Hummer was so pleased with the finished product that he told his friend about me, and that's how I found out about Greg "Coach Roz" Roeszler, Founder and Executive Director of the Playmakers Mentoring Foundation [www.ThePlaymakers.org].

Two weeks after I finished the letter for Hummer, my phone rang. Roz had called to thank me. As with Hummer, we hit it off right away. The stories he told me about the kids he serves were so touching, I said I hoped he was writing them down. "Well, Miss Donna, I'm pretty good at talking, but not very good at writing."

Without giving it any thought at all, I heard myself saying, "Well, if you need any help, let me know."

"Oh, Miss Donna, I don't want to cause you any trouble." He paused, then, "But I could tape some of them and you could just listen."

"Yes, do that. I'd like to hear them." Of course, once I heard the stories, I knew he had a book, so that's how our first book, *Coaching for a Bigger Win, A Playbook for Coaches*, began. [Other books are currently being developed. Omaha now has a full-fledged Playmakers Chapter, too, complete with its own Captain's Club (their mentoring arm), free summer youth football camps, and annual fund raisers.]

A short time later, Roz asked me how Hummer and I had met, so I told him our story. "But when did you actually *meet* him?" Roz found it difficult to believe Hummer and I could be such good friends when we'd never even met, so it wasn't long before Roz invited me to meet him at the Las Vegas airport so we could go and see Hummer. Roz told Hummer he was coming to town "on business" and wondered if he could stop by. He didn't tell Hummer I was coming, too.

When I first saw Roz at the baggage claim, I was struck by the beauty of his spirit. Like sunlight through a stained-glass window, his spirit just shines right through. We hugged and laughed and even cried a little as we rejoiced over the adventure we were on together.

Later, as we approached Hummer's home, we were excited beyond belief. Even though he hadn't seen Hummer for thirty years, it was easy to see how much Roz still loved and admired this great man. When we were about a mile away, Roz called Hummer and told him he was bringing him a present.

"Leave it in the car!" was Hummer's quick response. "I don't need any presents!"

"Sorry, old man. I can't do that, so get over it, okay?" Roz affectionately countered.

Finally we pulled up in front of the house. As we started walking toward the house, there sat Hummer in the doorway, saying over and over, "Oh my God! It's Donna! *Oh my God!*"

As with Roz, the sight of Hummer touched me to tears. His beautiful, sweet spirit just glows. Years ago, when I was recovering from serious back surgery, someone sent me a card that said, "Even when caged up, a bird still sings." It's a lot like that with Hummer. Even though MS has taken a great toll on his body, not only does his spirit sing, it soars. All you have to do is see him and you hear the song, you feel the light, you see the spirit shining through.

So how do you greet someone you have loved so fiercely for so long? Roz and I both just fell to our knees and the hugs and tears began.

We spent the afternoon sitting around the table and talking like three old buddies catching up on the news. After a while, Hummer's daughter, Courtney, arrived and the greetings started all over again. Courtney was eighteen then. I'd been seeing her pictures and following her stories since she was eight, but the pictures simply didn't do her justice. She has her father's same sweet spirit and, like her dad, it shines right through. Needless to say, the joy of the afternoon filled our hearts to overflowing, and it still does.

When the time came for us to leave, Hummer followed us to the door. More hugs. More expressions of love. More hugs again.

As we finally got in the car, Hummer was in the doorway waving goodbye, with Courtney standing right behind him. Smiling, waving, throwing kisses back and forth, we slowly pulled away.

As we approached the corner, a profound silence filled the car. I glanced at Roz through the tears in my eyes and saw he was struggling, too. I reached in my purse, pulled out a tissue and handed it to him.

"Thanks," was the hoarse reply.

"I need you to see so you can drive."

Somehow, nothing more needed to be said.

When Hummer asked me to check his letter for commas, I had no idea I was about to enter a totally different world from any I'd ever known. Oh yes, I've been to lots of football games. I've sat in the stands and cheered my heart out, but as I'm sure you already know, seeing is not the same as doing. I found that out when I went to visit Coach Roz and his family later that fall. The purpose of the trip was to meet his football team, talk with his coaches, and participate in every phase of what the Playmakers are doing.

From the study skills sessions, to watching the films, to the practice field, to the locker room, and to the game where they won for the first time in three years—I was there for it all. Feeling their energy, their excitement and anticipation, and even their anxiety, touched me clear through. I was impressed with how the kids all came up and introduced themselves at the first study skills session. As the days unfolded, we had many chances to talk one on one. Slowly we became friends.

On Thursday, I was there with them when they had lunch before we boarded the bus to go to the game. I listened to Roz and the other coaches as they gave their final talks to the kids, bolstering their courage, reminding them of what they must do to win, and also what they must do to be winners, regardless of the score.

There was a feeling in the locker room right before the game that cannot be described. It was so thick, so heavy, so strong, you could almost cut it with a knife. The faces, the energy, the excitement, the smells—it was all there. I reflected back to my days before an organ concert and my own anxiety, anticipation, focus, and concentration. I could see that in their faces now, too.

Sitting and waiting is the hardest part. The room was electric. It was palpable. You could feel it. And when you can finally get off that bench and go out onto the field, the juice really begins to flow. The tension is still there, but now it keeps you sharp. It keeps you focused. It energizes you and enables you to instinctively follow the commands and the calls and execute the plays you have learned.

I phoned Hummer right before the game. I wanted him to know where we were, what the field was like, how the boys were doing. "I'll call you tomorrow and let you know how it went," I said, and I really thought that would be the next time we would talk. Then we had the kick-off. That's when our excitement went off the scale, because the boys ran the opening kick back and scored on the very first play! Immediately I was on the phone. "We scored!"

"You're kidding!" was Hummer's reply.

"No, we ran the ball back! I'll call you later!" It didn't take long for "later" to come. We kicked to the other team, and on the next play we intercepted a pass and ran the ball in for another touchdown. Back on the phone. "We scored again!"

"No way!" was his incredulous reply.

"Yes, it's true!" I shouted into the phone. At this point I'm dancing and laughing, jumping up and down, and this continued over and over throughout the game, after every score, theirs or ours. I must have been quite a sight, as it was very cold at the field. I had at least six layers on, plus a team hat on top of my hood. Every time the kids came off the field, this grandma many times over was running up and down, thumping the kids on the back, praising them for what they did.

"Good for you!" "You really hung onto that ball!" "Way to go, #5!" "Great job! You sure hung in there!" Over and over. I may not have been carrying the ball, and I may not have been in uniform, but on that night, I was on that team.

Although we got off to a running start, it didn't take long for the other team to wake up. They started scoring, too. The problem, for them at least, was that we had over fifty boys on our team. The other team had only eighteen, so they were working really hard and, as sometimes happens, they got dehydrated and began cramping up. The first time this happened, the boy was on the ground right in front of our team.

"Get him some water," Coach Roz said to the water girl who was standing nearby.

"But, Coach, he's on the other team!"

Coach looked directly at her. *"Get him some water!"*

So that became the practice. Every time one of their players went down, our water girls were out there giving them some water. Yes, football does teach us life lessons, and not just to the players.

By halftime, the score was much too close. It was time to refocus, time to rethink what we're doing, to correct some things, to make some adjustments. The atmosphere in the locker room was intense. The kids' faces were serious, yet the coaches showed their confidence in what the kids could do. It was beautiful watching how these gentle men worked with the kids. It was like a machine, with every piece doing its own part.

So out we came for the second half, and it started all over again. The kids just scored and scored. The other team kept coming back, but always we were ahead. Then, as the clock ran down to just over six minutes, the score got close again. I called Hummer.

"Tell Roz to *run that clock!*" was his immediate response. And that's exactly what I did.

To the very end, we were all rooting, cheering, clapping, yelling, cracking helmets together. Finally the game ended, and we were still ahead. Whew!

What makes this so remarkable is that this team hadn't won a game in three years! The week before, their first game of the season, they scored twice, and that was pretty exciting! The fact that they lost really didn't matter, because they had scored twice. The previous year they didn't score at all until the sixth game, so all in all, they were ahead. And now this week, can you believe it, they came off the field with a 65–50 win! Amazing things can happen when once you believe.

Hearts were soaring. We were jumping up and down. Everybody was hugging everybody, and the kids kept coming over to say, "Thank you for coming! You brought us luck!"

"I didn't do it. You did it! You just didn't know you could," was my constant reply. "You can do this, and now you know that!"

The week before I flew to Sacramento, we had a guest speaker at our church who talked about how, when people gather together and emotions are engaged, bonding occurs. I thought about that as I was running up and down the sidelines, literally dancing in glee over each and every score, each and every wonderful thing the kids were doing. Yes, indeed, bonding does occur.

The next day at study skills, I had a chance to speak to the kids before Coach Roz began his talk. I told them how awesome they are, how proud of them I was, how far they've come, and how I know they are going to continue moving in this direction because they can do this. Now they know they can. I connected with every eye in that room, and they were looking straight back at me. It was truly a special moment.

After the coaches finished talking, we went out to the practice field for a light practice, "Just to keep us loose," Coach Roz said. When practice was over, the kids all got down on one knee for Roz's closing talk.

When he finished, he surprised me. "Is there anyone here who would like to be in a group picture with Miss Donna?" All the hands went up, so I went over and took the one-knee pose just like everybody else so we could get a picture of our football family.

To my surprise, when I stood up, they all gathered around me and raised their helmets for a helmet salute and cheer. They made a huge dome above me with their helmets. It touched me so, I was about in tears, and I am even now just thinking about it. When the helmets came down, the kids came over and every single one gave me a hug. That gave me a chance to speak to every one of these fifty-plus kids personally, to encourage them, to love and praise them.

Playmakers like to say, "We are family." I have to say, yes, indeed we are. To know these kids is to love them. To look at them, you would never know they have come through such difficult, difficult circumstances. Some of them are homeless, some of them parentless, some of them fatherless, and yet they persevere. Their courage is inspiring. They have been drawn together by the magnetism of Coach Roz and his team of dedicated coaches who truly believe that if kids are shown the way, if they are given the opportunity, there is no dream they cannot fulfill.

That's what being a Playmaker is all about. Through their football family, these kids are beginning to experience pride in their accomplishments, dignity and, for many of them, finding out for the first time what a family is all about.

Because of the kids' tenacity, because of their ability to carry on and not give up, they have been drawn to these men who hold this great vision. These coaches played football together as kids, and now they're coaching in the inner city together, guiding the boys into manhood. These men could coach anywhere, but they have chosen to coach these lost kids, and they are doing it together.

Friday night we drove to another town to scout the team they'd be playing the next week at Homecoming. The news was good. As we watched the team, we began to think there was a chance we might win our Homecoming game, too! Wouldn't that be something? Two games in a row! And Homecoming besides!

That possibility would certainly be something to build on during the coming week, and yet in our hearts, we know these kids are already winners, regardless of the score. They are ahead of the game. They are working their hearts out. They are learning how to give their best effort. They are developing self-confidence. They have found out how to care about each other, and what that means. The score doesn't get any better than that!

Sunday morning, on the way to church, we drove over to the most dangerous part of the city to watch the youth football teams Coach Zo and his wife, Dee Dee, have put together. Precious little children, as young as seven and eight, came marching onto the field in full uniform, filled with pride and excitement.

They were led onto the field by a full complement of cheerleaders—little girls who didn't come up to my waist, but there they were, also in full costume, complete with pompoms. As we watched them cheering the boys on, just like the girls in high school, I found myself giving thanks for people who dedicate their lives to showing these children a way out of the inner city, people who want nothing other than to give the children hope. People like Roz and Zo and Dee Dee and so many others are like lights shining in the night for these kids.

Roz put it so well. "If we can provide a vehicle that bridges the gap for those little kids, if there are programs and mechanisms in place that keep those kids accountable and give them direction, then we're not going to lose them. Then, by the time they get to high school, we won't have some of the problems we're facing now. We're showing them a way out of the inner city so they can have a better way of life."

Amen to that! Amen, and again, Amen!

When you've never known your father, how can you know what a father should act like? When you've never had a family, how can you know what that means? And when you've had to fend for yourself all your young life, to whom can you look for a role model? Who is there to teach you what it means to have real character, to be responsible, and, yes, to take care of yourself and others, too? How does one learn to be a good citizen, even a leader in the community, when your entire life has been based on survival?

This is the predicament so many of our young people face, but because there are those who care, a way out is being carved in the streets and slums of our inner cities. Because there are those who care, a "family" is being formed where kids can feel safe, where they are not only respected but loved. In the shelter of these "families," coaches who care stand both as role models and surrogate fathers for these lost children. As they do, they teach the kids what community service means, so they can learn to reach beyond themselves.

As the kids learn how to serve, a sense of pride and responsibility and, yes, leadership begins to grow in their young hearts. Now they can hold their heads up high. Because now they know why there are rules, abiding by those rules becomes a source of pride. Now they know it is by working together that they can all succeed. And when one of them happens to stray, as we all do at some time or other, the lessons of leadership and compassion take on real meaning for those young compatriots who help them find their way back.

Integrity becomes a word with meaning, a word that defines how they are trying to live their life. Integrity becomes the gold standard for these budding citizens, for they are learning through their own experience that those who live with integrity live well, regardless of the circumstances in which life has placed them.

Because the kids are trying, because they are sincere, dreams begin to form. "Maybe I can go to college someday. If I work hard enough, maybe that will be possible."

"No," the coaches tell them. "Not maybe. You *will*. If you can dream it, you can do it," and so the dream grows. Horizons broaden. Their world and their vision are no longer confined by the streets of the inner city, no longer threatened by gang rule. They have found a way out, because someone cared.

Unfortunately, too many of our youth are caught in this maze, but the good news is that people who care are doing something about it all over the nation. Mentoring groups are springing up wherever you turn. Coaches are dedicating their lives to providing shelter and guidance for those who need it. The wheel is turning slowly, but it is turning. Lives are being changed. Dreams are being realized. More and more we all are learning that life is about helping each other.

When you care about someone else, you make a difference that cannot be measured. This is what Playmakers is all about. I speak from the heart when I say it is an honor to be among them.

You'll Never Be Surprised

Listen closely,
For I have something to tell you,
Something to whisper in your ear!
Fill your dreams with
Impossible things,
And every chance you get,
Imagine the improbable!
If you do,
You'll never be surprised
Because the unlikely
Will become your reality,
And all you'll want to do is smile.

TWENTY FIVE

Accepting the Divine Design

*"Walk your path with courage so you
can live the life you were born to live."*

To this day, I marvel at how all the pieces of my life just fell
in place. This has been an adventure far beyond anything I
could have imagined. From that first clue when the letter from the
Board of Christian Outreach arrived to what I am doing now with
at-risk youth, it's almost as though there was a divine design to it.
And maybe there was.

If someone had asked me twenty years ago what I thought I
would be doing now, I have to confess my answer would have been
nowhere close to where I am. I think life is like that for most of
us. We make plans, but life does not always listen to our plans. Life
has plans of its own. While we may not always welcome what life
brings, there is one thing of which we can be certain—whatever
life brings, it always comes bearing a gift. I know I've said this
before, but it is true. It may be a while before we find the gift, but it
is there. Finding the gift is part of the journey. I never thought that
would apply to the "separation" that comes with death, but it does.

All my life I've watched others live with grief and sorrow. To a
large extent their loss became their identity, but I found I could
not do that. I knew I had to let go of the pain that grief wants to
impose if I was going to move on with my life in a way that would
honor those who had gone on before me. It was a gradual, but
necessary, process.

Eventually I realized I did not need the pain any longer. Moving beyond the pain allowed me to see what I still have, what I never lost at all. The wonderful, indescribable, nurturing love we shared expanded and resolved into a presence that filled my days. In changing form, our love became even more. Day by day I grew into the realization that our time together here was just the beginning, that the best is yet to come, and all that follows will be an expansion of that love.

Accepting the inevitable and making peace with it enables you to find a Way when there does not seem to be a way. It allows you to reach for the heights even while your spirit is at the depths of its grief. Accepting life on its own terms makes it possible not only to move on, to find new meaning and purpose for your life, but to do so knowing that all is not lost, only changed. While that change can be shattering, strength can be forged from the crucible of our grief as we learn that death is never the end, but rather a beginning.

Yes, it is the beginning of a new chapter in which we discover that the relationships that helped make us what we are have not ended at all. Indeed, they have become richer through this new dimension in which they now must find expression. Now we see that the cycles that may seem to separate us are but the cycles of our evolution. As we seek the means and the will to continue, so, too, do we find new meaning and a new perspective from which we can live our life. This perspective enables us to face death, even our own death, with a serenity and peace that is born of the knowledge that all is well, and all shall be well, even when life has been turned upside down, and all is changed beyond recognition.

The Mystery

I dwell in the
Mystery of the
Great Unknown
Fluid, beautiful and free.

I dance with the wind
And relish each breath
Ecstatic each day
Just to be.

I sing with the joy
Of the planets and stars,
I laugh with the waves
And the sea,

For I am the spirit
Forever unfolding
Unbounded, eternal
And free.

TWENTY SIX

Reflections

"All things come in their own time."

As long as I can remember, I've been aware of my own spirituality. I just seemed to know I was more than "just" this body. As a child at church, I remember listening and wondering why they didn't think like I did. I don't recall ever expressing those thoughts to my elders. The opinions of children were not in favor back in those times. It was frustrating, because there was so much I wanted to say, even more that I wanted to ask, but I just kept my thoughts and my beliefs to myself.

Imagine my relief when, at the age of seventeen, I was introduced to meditation! *Finally*, someone else knew what I knew, and so the trek began. The meditation practice I learned was a start, but it wasn't enough. Years went by as I continued my search for the key that would open the "door" to my soul. I read books, attended workshops and classes, practiced every form of meditation I could find, to no avail.

When I finally found out about Deepak and David and Roger, the key began to turn. Primordial Sound Meditation (PSM)—the practice they taught—was literally the light at the end of the tunnel for me. Doors began to open, windows opened wide, and nothing has been the same ever since.

Looking back, I don't know how I would have survived had it not been for PSM. It kept me afloat during one of the most difficult periods of my life and allowed my healing to begin in earnest. I began to find my way through my grief as I learned how to cope with all the changes that were coming into my life.

The most immediate challenge was finding a sense of identity. I had spent all my life thus far being what others needed me to be, which, in all truth, was probably what I needed to be at the time. But once my husband was gone, what was I then? *Who* was I then? Slowly the realization came that it was time to be myself. I didn't yet know what that was, or even what shape it would take, but I gave myself permission to follow my heart. Once I made that commitment, I never looked back.

The Chopra Center's courses were so nurturing, so healing at such deep levels. It seemed every course they offered had been designed just for me. It was at one of their courses in our beloved La Jolla that Roger Gabriel led us through a meditation where I spontaneously moved into another space. I found myself down by the ocean (which was actually only three blocks away and which I frequented every chance I got), but this time it was different.

As we moved through the meditation, I found myself being the seagull flying over the ocean. As I (the seagull) looked down at the water, suddenly I "became" the water. Looking around, I saw a fish, and then I was the fish. After a short while, I looked toward the shore and felt myself, as the ocean, splashing on the shore. I felt myself playing with the shore, throwing my waves against her glistening sand, frolicking with her, laughing at the pure joy of the moment.

The next thing I knew, I was the beach, too, the warm, sandy beach. I turned, and saw the beautiful cliffs that looked over the sand and the beach and the ocean, and then I was the cliffs. I'll never forget being those cliffs, how they were quietly, peacefully observing the play of wind and water, fish and fowl. It was then I realized that even the cliffs were conscious! Even the cliffs were aware! Awareness was everywhere—and so was I!

Roger had some music playing in the background, and when the music changed, I found myself moving out into space to the stars and planets. I was so disappointed when the music stopped and the meditation ended. I wanted to be there forever, but even though I had to "come back," the memory stayed with me. I was beginning to understand, in a completely new way, that I was so much more than just this body.

Scanning the galaxies under the direction of Dr. David Morehouse confirmed even more that I had just begun to scratch the surface of who and what I am—of what we all are, for that matter.

It happened again when I was on tour in India with Roger Gabriel. We had just arrived at a lovely resort by the Arabian Sea. I was so excited. I could hardly wait to walk to the beach by the sea. As I came over the crest of a dune, the wide expanse unfolded before me, and there, right in front of me, an ancient fishing boat passed by, just like those that have been used for thousands of years. It could have been any moment in time. Surrendering completely to that timeless moment, I gave myself to the sea and the shore and sky, letting that vast expanse enfold me completely.

Later, as I walked back to my cottage, I came across a barren tree in the sand. There were other trees like it that had many leaves, but this tree had no leaves at all. Instead, at the very end of the farthest branch were some of the most beautiful blossoms I had ever seen. What a message that was for me! As I stood there reverently communing with that tree, I sensed how, for whatever reasons, it wasn't able to put out leaves, so it chose instead to offer these few blossoms to the sun. Its message touched me deeply, and I thought to myself, *I just hope, when life is difficult, and there is so little in the outer to draw upon, that I can do as this barren tree has, and create something beautiful.*

This was just the beginning, of course. More and more, inexplicable events came into my life, reinforcing an inner conviction that what we "see" is only the tip of the iceberg. Our true reality is so much deeper than that. And so the days and weeks and years went by. Slowly I was growing and finding the peace I so hungered for.

I read recently that many times our serious spiritual work doesn't begin until life puts us in a position where we have no choice. Dr. David Hawkins says when that time comes, we're either going to go up or go down. He is right. It was definitely sink or swim for me.

I've never been a very good swimmer, but I was learning. The crises that confronted me forced me into a time of becoming. Of growing. Of finding the new, and, yes, the miraculous right here in my daily life.

One of the most miraculous experiences for me was finding out that we are loved—and accepted—so fully, so completely that there is nothing left to forgive! This is true for all of us, and that is why I'm sharing my story, because the challenges I've faced are universal. We all have our mountains to climb, both inner and outer. No one is exempt.

Life is a school, and what we learn through that school are the lessons we are ready for, things we could not really know until we lived through them. I'm talking about experiential knowledge, not just head knowledge. "They" say you don't really know something until you become it. "They" are right. And that is how I found out that relationships change, but they do not end. Physical death is definitely not the end of the story.

Our trials and tribulations are so rich with promise. It may not seem like it at the time, but they are. Nothing is ever wasted. The potential for growth—and new life—is hidden in even the most difficult of situations. *Especially* in the most difficult ones, because all things do indeed come bearing a gift, if we can just hang in there long enough to find it.

It helps if we can accept and embrace what is. That means being open enough to let go of judgment—of yourself, and others, and even the challenge itself. It means letting go of our expectations so we can be open to the higher plan. Surrender fits well here. Not my will, but Thine.

Eventually, you find out that your life isn't just about you. It's about all of us. That means wanting for others the same things we yearn for so deeply. May we *all* be blessed.

As I said earlier, it's been quite a journey. The more I've learned, the more I realize how far I still have to go, but this much I know: life isn't about "things." It's about be-ing—being your highest and best, and that journey never ends.

Now, as I look back, I think Neal knew we were on the cusp. We'd loved each other fully and completely through thick and thin—and there was a lot of both, with all his physical challenges. We'd taken each other as far as we could, and probably as far as his physical body would allow. Now we were both ready to move into a larger way of being. It was time for both of us to spread our wings and fly. Of course, I didn't see that then, but I do now. In fact, I can't help wondering if perhaps this was the plan long before we found each other, and that's why I think Neal knew this was coming.

That last year especially, there were so many times when Neal said he wanted to buy me something, but what did I want? All I could answer was, "I only want you, honey." He must have known how short the time was getting, but he never said so. He just lived each day wishing there was one last thing he could do for me.

Well, he got his wish. What I've learned has been the greatest gift of all.

TWENTY SEVEN

Tuning In to the Stillness

*"Learning to go where words cannot go
is the greatest gift you can give yourself."*

Last night we had a violent storm—high wind, heavy rain, even hail. The contrast between how noisy it was outside and yet how silent, how very still it was inside was almost palpable. As I listened, I found myself thinking about how the stillness is always here, even in the midst of a storm. You just have to know how to find it.

There are so many ways to savor the stillness. One of my favorite ways is to sit on the porch at the close of the day and listen to the children play. It's fun to watch them. They are so spontaneous and free. I've even learned to be comfortable with the level of noise they create, which sometimes is just short of a sonic boom, or so it seems. Then, after they've all gone home, the sweetness of the memories and the comfort of the silence somehow fuse together, creating a smile that lingers on my face.

As I sit there and relish the quiet, the contrast between their presence and their absence is profound. At first it seems more like the absence of noise. Only later, when I've had a chance to settle into the quiet, do I become aware that there is something deeper here, something that has its roots in the depths of my being, something I long to touch with all my heart.

That's the message contrast offers, I think. Contrast, particularly great contrast, is nearly always profound, isn't it? Whether we're talking about silence, or life, or love and all their opposites, contrast continually brings substance to our experience and meaning to our days.

Of course, if we really want to experience the silence, we have to learn to quiet our mind. That's where most of the noise is, it seems. To do that requires shifting our attention away from all of our busy thoughts. I do this best when I meditate.

When I first began meditating, my goal was to quiet my mind. I've since learned that meditating is far more than that. It's about becoming aware. Not awareness *of* something, but simply learning to *be aware*. The deeper your awareness, the more profound the silence. When you are truly aware, you consciously enter into the stillness that underlies all creation. That stillness is your essential nature. It is the very fabric of your soul.

Of course, when you begin meditating, the mind does not want to release its hold on you. It continually offers things to think about, things to do, things you should attend to now, things the mind thinks cannot wait. Reminders especially have a way of cropping up at the beginning of meditation, at least they do for me. "Oh! You forgot to do this!" or "Oh! You *must* do that!" Of course, the impulse is to get up and do them. The discipline is in saying, "No. Not now. Later."

Once the mind understands that you aren't going to get up and do it now, that it really must quiet down, there is still the body to contend with. The body, too, has its needs, so patiently, level by level, we start to relax. Gradually, we settle in to a quieter state. As we do, the breathing gets quieter, the thoughts fewer until, almost without our knowing it, an awareness develops within us. Like the fragrance of a rose, without our ever knowing where it came from, we slip into the part of us that is. This is the part of us that is always quiet, that always sees, always knows, is never sick, does not die. Some call it the witness, others call it the soul, and some call it the Self. Even though we try to give it a name, it is the nameless aspect of our being. It cannot be described, nor can it be defined.

When you are truly in the silence, all that does not matter. Just to be *There*, just to be immersed in the awareness of *That* fills us with a peace and a joy beyond description.

If we are attentive, if we surrender to the process, gradually we find ourselves totally absorbed, totally caught up in this pure consciousness until finally we move beyond the mind altogether into a state that can only be described as Is-ness. Here we touch upon a way of being that is so pure, so deep that we realize there is nothing else, only *This*. Then we know, just as the ancient sages did, that That's all there is. There simply is no other.

After a while, as we continue offering ourselves to these depths, we notice how that same presence, that same inner silence begins appearing not just when we meditate, but in our daily life, too. Our pace becomes more sane, our mind not so frantic. Even our patience seems to have gained a new dimension. In ways both large and small, the truth of our being, of our very nature, begins to seep into our lives at every level. We find we're not as easily upset. We laugh more. Our perspective seems broader, more mellow. Life just doesn't seem so frantic anymore.

These changes are signs that the alchemy is at work. I'm talking about the alchemy that happens deep within us as we become the peace we were seeking. Much like a wave of energy in a great mystical ocean, the silence moves through us and flows out into our days. It's easier to relax now, for somehow we know that all is as it should be, whether it seems so or not. We trust and we smile, for we know that love is having its way with us. We are content, because love's way is all we could have hoped for, all we could have asked.

More and more, we begin to tune into that ineffable otherness that underlies all our daily-ness. We notice it when we're walking, or doing the dishes, or driving down the street. It's just always there.

If this is so, then why didn't we see it before? Why aren't we in touch with it now? Could it be because we aren't looking? Because we aren't paying attention? Because we simply aren't aware?

So where is the silence for you today? Can you feel it between your thoughts? Between your words? Your actions? Can you rest in it? Can you taste the sense of be-ing that underlies all that you are? Can you feel it move you? Guide you?

If you haven't connected with the silence lately, just stop what you are doing—right now—and listen. Just be aware...

If you practice the stillness often enough, that awareness will become part of the fabric of your life. Being still inwardly will become as natural to you as breathing or eating or sleeping. When it is, you'll be more alert to its promptings, and you'll trust more.

So practice being aware. Just *be* every chance you can. Your deepest truths have their being in the silence of your heart.

And so do you.

Learning to Meditate

So how does one find the peace one is seeking? For me, the answer was through meditation.

Although there are many ways to meditate, the practice that allowed me to reach into my depths where peace resides was Primordial Sound Meditation, but whatever form you use, it's important to begin with something that is comfortable for you. All forms are valid, and they all have a purpose, so find the method that works for you. If you are faithful in your practice, your quiet times will become a haven, a safe place where you can always go.

When you do meditate, it's important to let the body be comfortable so it doesn't distract you. If that means sitting in a chair, fine. If you prefer lotus position with your legs crossed on the floor, that's fine, too. If you can, having your back straight offers support and lets the breath flow more easily.

Unless the meditation directs you to lie down on the floor, sitting up is what is usually recommended. You'll also want to be in a quiet place whenever possible so you can more fully experience your meditation.

If you've never meditated before, guided meditations can be a good way to begin. If you're already meditating but are having some difficulty working through your present challenges, the guided meditations that follow might be of some help to you. Each one begins with a short introduction, followed by the meditation itself. At the end of the meditation, there will be some questions for you to consider as you integrate your experience.

If you would like, you could record these meditations ahead of time, making sure you leave the space you need to experience whatever is suggested. Or you can just read through them slowly and silently, giving yourself the time you want to fully experience the meditation, pausing to consider what was just said whenever you see "…"

Finding the Gift that Adversity Brings

INTRO: Life is a school. Change—especially great change— can be the bearer of many lessons. Our most difficult challenges almost always are our most important teachers. If we don't learn the lesson this time, it will come again in another form. The good news is, once you have learned a lesson, you don't ever have to learn it again.

Adversity does shape and define us in ways that nothing else can. In God's economy, nothing is ever wasted. All things come bearing a gift, so be faithful to the call when it comes and know it really is possible to overcome even this.

So just take a minute now to get comfortable … And when you are settled in your chair, let's begin by taking a deep breath … As you breathe in, breathe in Peace … and on the exhale, just let go of any stresses you may have brought with you … Now let's breathe in again, and this time, breathe in Light … on the exhale, just let that Light flow into every part of your being … And now let's breathe in Love … On the exhale, send that Love out to all sentient beings …

Today we're going to focus on finding the gift that adversity brings … Whenever you wonder why something has come into your life, know there is a lesson you are ready for, and this is the form in which it has come …

While we are not given a choice in how these lessons come, we do have a choice in how we respond, so just take a moment to think about how you are responding to what is going on in your life ... Now if you can, choose to be a conscious choice maker ... One way to do that is to simply ask yourself, "What is this trying to teach me? What can I learn from this?" You might want to do that even now ...

And if you are struggling with something, chances are you are resisting it. So take a deep breath right now, and on the exhale, see if you can let go of any anxiety or concern you might have ... See if you can find a way to begin accepting what is happening in your life ...

Acceptance is a very important tool. Acceptance leads to the way out. Acceptance helps you see things as they are, and gives you the perspective you need to see what you can or cannot change ... Acceptance makes it easier to let go. To let be what will be. To not get hung up on results. To trust that whatever happens really is for the best. Can you do that now? ... Yes, we're talking about surrender, and surrender can open up a deep source of strength when the going gets rough ...

You see, it really is possible to teach your mind what you want it to do. This is important, because then you'll be able to draw a line beyond which you are not willing to go. You'll know when you are approaching deep water, and you'll consciously choose not to go where you do not want to swim. Instead, being a conscious choice maker, you'll focus on what you do want, so you can bring more of that quality into your experience. So ask yourself now, what quality would you like to have more of in your daily life? ... Is there a way you can help that happen? ...

Your heart already knows the answer. If you are quiet, if you are open, the answers will come. So for just a moment now, bring your attention to your heart ... Listen to your heart ... Your heart always knows, and it will guide you. It will send you signals—signals of comfort or discomfort—that will lead you along your path ...

It will help if you can find time in your daily life to consciously connect with the peace and stillness that are the very ground of your being ... Then, if you can, bring that stillness into your every thought and feeling ... Day after patient day, integrate that stillness and that peace into your daily living and see the difference it makes ...If you do, you may even notice a Presence that is always with you. Can you feel it? ... The faithfulness of that Presence just may open a door—a way of seeing—that you've never known before. You may even begin to sense that same Presence in others, too. You may see that same living, loving Presence looking back at you everywhere you go. When that happens, you will know you are never really alone, no matter what ... That knowing creates a confidence and fortitude that will help carry you through other difficult times ... Then, regardless of what else is happening in your life, you can still rest in that beautiful, loving Presence you have come to know during your quiet times ...

This kind of acceptance, this kind of freedom, is very healing. It allows you to use your pain as a means of growth. It allows you to see through your challenge to one of the greatest gifts it offers—Who You Really Are. Just take a moment and think about Who You Really Are right now ...

So day after day simply, humbly practice being Who You Really Are. In all the little daily things, affirm the truths on which you are hanging the sum total of your faith. Then you'll begin to understand that your thoughts, your life, and even your death are just stages in your journey. You'll know for yourself that there is no darkness. There is only Light, and it is everywhere ...

More and more, you'll begin to see that the fabric of your life is one uncut, unbroken whole ... Now you'll know that you are whole, regardless of what else may be going on ... In that moment of silent understanding, all your fears will slip away as quietly as they came ...

So just give yourself another moment now to consider these things ... and when you are ready, slowly open your eyes.

1. In looking back over your life, can you see any lessons you have learned from previous challenges?

2. Can you also see the gift—the blessing—that came with those challenges?

3. Have you ever sensed signals of comfort or discomfort in your heart? Were you willing to follow those leadings? If not, why not?

Learning to Let Go

INTRO: One of the reasons our challenges can be so difficult is because we are resisting them. It is only human to want to be in control, but when we try to do that, we end up with two problems instead of one. Whenever we try to control what's happening in our life, we limit the possibilities.

It isn't easy to let go. The unknown can be scary. Sometimes we think we know what's best when actually there may be a better plan at work that we just aren't aware of yet. The unknown holds the greatest potential for our good. Being open to that best possible outcome is a way of life that can be developed, so for today's meditation, let's see if we can learn how to let go.

Give yourself the time you need to get comfortable, perhaps even taking a few deep breaths, releasing any stress you might be feeling on the exhale, and when you are ready, slowly close your eyes …

For just a moment now, imagine that you are walking down to a boat that is sitting at the edge of a river … As you walk to the river's edge, you see your boat sitting there … It doesn't have to be a big boat, just whatever feels comfortable for you to sail on. The sight of it is very inviting …

The current of the river represents your life and where it would like to take you … all the things that life has in store for you … your hopes and dreams … even things you haven't yet thought of … you know they are all there in the course of that river …

You also know that if you are to engage with all these wonderful experiences, you are going to have to get in that boat, so let's do that now. If you can, just see yourself climbing into the boat … It may rock a little as you do that, but that's okay … As you are climbing in, you recognize that if the boat is going to take you anywhere, you're going to have to put both feet in the boat … You can't go anywhere with one foot on the shore and one foot in the boat. If you put both feet in the boat, you must be willing to let go of the familiar, of all the things you've known and trusted … That's what sailing into the unknown requires … but you really want this kind of freedom … You want to be able to disengage from the past and all its limitations so you can set out for new horizons … so say a word of thanks for all that has brought you this far … and with one last glance toward the shore, turn toward the river and put both feet in the boat. Give yourself all the time you need to do this …

Once you are in the boat, you realize there is one more thing you must do … You must "pull anchor" and push off from the shore. As long as the anchor is down, your boat isn't going to go anywhere … Just take a moment to think about what this means … Pulling anchor means committing yourself to the journey … It means being willing to go wherever the river takes you … It means trusting that the current of the river, which is really the current of your lifestream, knows exactly where you need to go … It knows exactly what you must do to become what you are meant to be … It knows exactly what must happen for you to fulfill your deepest heart's desires … So pull up the anchor and push off from the shore. Give yourself the time you need to do that now …

Ever so gently, the boat moves out into the river … As it slides into the current easily and effortlessly, you sit in your boat and feel the breeze on your face and in your hair … and in your heart you are smiling … You feel in sync with the universe and its plan for you … It is a comfortable feeling, so you are content to let the river have its way with you … Powers greater and wiser than yours are steering your boat now … and you are content to trust them …

As you sit there in your boat, you notice a set of oars nearby ...
It would be tempting to take the oars in your hands and help steer
the boat, but something inside you tells you that you'll never get
where you're supposed to go if you do that, so you just smile and
leave the oars where they are ...

You see now that your life is your boat ... If you have truly made
this commitment, wherever you are, whatever you are doing, you
will still be in your boat ... This might be a good time to promise
yourself that you will trust the process ... that you will let your inner
guide steer you through all the things that fill your days ... If you
can, just take a moment and do that now ... You might even want to
offer a prayer of gratitude for all the good that awaits you ...

Now, having done that, ever so gently begin coming back to this
time ... and this place ... and this room ... and this moment ...
And when you are ready, slowly open your eyes.

1. Is there something in your life that you have been resisting?
2. Is there any part of that situation that you feel you can let
   go of?
3. Are you willing to open yourself to the higher plan that is
   trying to work itself out in your life?
4. What one thing can you do to energize that intention right
   now?

Befriending Your Growing Edge

INTRO: Whether we know it or not, we create the situations that will teach us the lessons we are ready for. Always the lessons are about love. Even the obstacles we encounter along the way were put there by our own creative spirit, but their ultimate purpose is always about love. To remove those obstacles, we must grow into a deeper understanding that will help us rise above them.

It is important to remember that whatever we encounter in life has a spiritual purpose behind it. As long as we are learning the lesson, the situation will be there. Once the lesson is learned, once we no longer need the situation, it will go as silently as it came.

All things happen in their own time. The higher our vision, the closer we will come to Spirit's purpose for us. We're really talking about tuning in to the higher purpose that is already within us. That higher purpose beckons much like a radio beam or homing signal. Spirit never stops sending signals of its intent to us, but it speaks to us silently, in our heart.

Learning to recognize Spirit's voice in our daily life is one of our most important lessons. In today's meditation, let's see if we can move beyond the boundaries to which we have become accustomed. Let's see if we can discover our silent inner world.

We're going to go on an exploration now, so this would be a good time to get comfortable in your chair. If you have recorded this meditation, you might even want to lie down on the floor. Just do whatever you need to do so you can be totally relaxed, because this is a journey of the mind. We don't want to have to think about the body for a while, so give yourself the time you need to get ready to do that now …

Once you are settled, once you are comfortable, I'd like you to take a few deep breaths. As you breathe in, breathe in Peace … and as you breathe out, just relax and release all your cares and concerns … The universe knows what you need, so if you can, just let go of any anxious feelings you might have as you prepare for your journey … Now close your eyes and do that again—breathe in Peace … breathe out any cares and concerns … breathe in Peace … breathe out all your tension … and once more, breathe in Peace … breathe out and relax clear down to the depths of your being …

Now as you rest in this quiet, peaceful place, you may notice that at the edge of your awareness there is a path … This is the path of your imagination, and we're going to follow it. Just take a minute to find that path, because it's going to take you to your very favorite place … It might be at the beach … It could be a meadow … Perhaps a cabin in the woods … Just follow your path to some quiet place where you can begin your journey …

Once you are there, you'll want to find a place to rest your body, a place where it can wait for you as you move into the inner reaches of your mind … So settle your body into that comfortable place where it can wait for you …

Once your body is settled, I'd like you to give yourself permission to enter the spaceship of your imagination, because we're going to begin moving away … We're going to start floating out into space … Your body is still resting in its comfortable place, and as you move away, you see it getting farther and farther away … Soon all you can see is your special place … and the countryside around it … until even that, too, begins to fade away … and this continent comes into view … then the oceans and seas of this wonderful planet … You see all of this as you move farther and farther away into the silent space of your imagination …

Farther and farther you go … away beyond the clouds … Look! Do you see … the moon is getting closer! … You marvel at the wonder of it, of seeing it so close ... You turn and look at Mother Earth ... See how beautiful she is ... how very special she is ...

Now with a deep sense of appreciation, you turn toward the stars ... toward that vast, unending sky ... You marvel at the harmony, the beauty, the intelligence here ... What feelings does this create in you? ... Is the cosmos speaking to you in some special way? ... Perhaps there is something you'd like to say. If there is, do so silently now as you move through the silent space within you ...

You are going even farther now ... stars go by ... whole galaxies come into view ... You pass by the galaxies like ships in the night ... Truly, this is a wondrous thing ... and it is all happening inside you ... in the vast reaches of your imagination ... and you realize that somehow the universe has its existence within you ... just as you have your existence in it ... and you ponder this now ...

As you continue your exploration, as you move inward through the vast inner space of your mind, you look around ... What else can you see here in this boundless realm ... for this mind of yours is a veritable storehouse of unimagined treasures ...

There are forms and figures here ... barest outlines ... some more complete than others ... Do you see them? ... These are your very own thought forms ... and they are growing within you! ... They are gathering substance ... gathering energy ... so they, too, can emerge and become part of your physical experience ...

This is the growing edge within you ... and these forms, these experiences that are taking shape within you are your very own creation ... So take a good look, for you have been given a gift ... You are being given the opportunity to decide whether or not you really want these experiences to manifest in your life ... whether or not you really want to experience these thoughts, these emotions, these intentions ... You are grateful that you have such a choice ... You can change this inner world of yours ... You can make it match the deepest desires of your heart ... and so you do that now ... As you walk through your inner gallery, look your thought forms over carefully ... and change whatever you'd like ... for you are shaping the forces at work in your life even now ...

Here, at this deep level of your mind, this is where your dreams take on substance ... This is your own creative space ... In this space you can be whatever you'd like to be ... You can do whatever you'd like to do, here, in your own inner space ... Just spend some time being and doing that now. Take all the time you need ...

This is your place of inner knowing ... It is your place of pure potential ... Help can always be found here, in the silent reaches of your being, for this is where your answers are ... So just take a moment to listen to the silence now... Is there something it wants you to know? ... Is there something it wants to tell you? ... Just be with the silence ... If you can, try to hear what it is saying ... Is it about the purpose of your life? ... Perhaps some insight about this phase of your journey? ...

This would be a good time to make a commitment to yourself, a promise of some kind, about the choices you'll be making ... the path you'll be following ... the way you want to use this earth opportunity ... Just listen to your heart, and let this time be whatever you want it to be ...

It's been quite a journey ... Just take a minute to reflect on all you have seen and done ... You know now that all this is what you are ... the atoms and molecules that make up your body ... the stars, the moons, the galaxies, the space ... and yes, the thought forms that have yet to emerge from within you ... this is all you ... How very special you are ... to have all this within you! ... And it is yours to use any way you'd like ... All the resources you need are within you ... and they ride on the in-breath and out-breath of your existence ...

So let's take one last look at your amazing inner space ... Say whatever you haven't yet said ... and when you've done that, just allow yourself to begin slowly rising to the surface ... Just allow the forms and shapes in your inner gallery to fade away ... until once again you are aware of your body as your own personal garment ...

Now take a slow, deep breath as you take up residence again in this amazing universe ... this universe that is so much a part of you ... And with yet another deep breath, allow yourself to become even more aware of your surroundings ... of this room ... this time ... this place ... and finally, when you are ready, and only when you are ready, slowly open your eyes.

1. Did you experience your own silent inner world during this meditation, and was it comfortable for you?
2. Were you able to see how your thoughts create your experience?
3. Can you see a spiritual purpose, perhaps even a lesson, in what is happening in your life right now?

Listening to Your Spirit

INTRO: We are so much more than this physical body. We are the Infinite Spirit expressing Itself through this physical body, and we are here for a purpose. We may not always be aware of that purpose, but whether we are or not, that purpose is working itself out through us.

In today's meditation, we seek to expand our awareness of Who We Are and Why We Are Here so we can participate more consciously in the unfolding of our life's purpose.

To begin our meditation, I'd like you to find a place where you can sit comfortably ... And when you are settled, just take a few deep breaths to clear out any stress you might be feeling ... Slowly breathe in and out, releasing whatever you need to let go of ...

Once you feel settled, just turn your attention to the silence that is everywhere all around you ... Notice how it has no edges, no beginnings or endings. Notice how the silence just IS ... Know that this is the Silence of Pure Being ... the very Source of life ... In that Silence is the potential for All That Is ... and as that All, it is your Source, even the very essence of your being ... So allow yourself now to settle into that field of silence, into your Source ... Breathe it ... Feel it ... Hear it ... BE it ...

Now as you rest in the Allness of this Presence, know that this Silence, this Presence, is on a journey of soul making, and the soul it is making is you ... All that is going on in the outer has its place in the scheme of things, but the real work, the most important work, is going on inside you ... for you are in a process of becoming, and what you are becoming is much more grand and wonderful than you can possibly imagine ...

There is no one else quite like you in all the universe ... for there is something you can do that no one else can do quite like you can ... You may not know yet what that something is, but it is there, in your heart ... Like a seed, the potential is in your heart ... and it is there for a reason ... it is there to fulfill a very special need ...

As you learn to listen to your heart, and follow its guidance, you will become aware of what your deepest heart's desire is ... That desire is the gift you are bringing to life ... In the giving of that gift is all the joy you could ever want ... all the happiness you could possibly ask for ... for this is a gift from the Infinite Source of all creation ... even the very Source that is creating and expressing Itself through you ...

So listen now ... Just rest in the silence and be very still ... Know that your guide is within you ... Your guide is always within you, here in your heart ...

Whenever you feel the need for clarity, simply ask, "How can I help? How can I serve?" and then rest in the silence. Perhaps you would like to do so now ...

Dear Soul, know that you are loved with a love beyond description, for you are the very Self of the Divine ... even the Eternal Spirit ... You dance with the stars and rise with the morning sun ... and even as you travel here, on this tiny planet, there is a part of you that sees and knows that you are on a journey of soul making ... Where you are going, and what you will be doing will unfold of its own accord ... for your mission is part of the great cosmic plan ...

So as you continue upon your journey, remember always to reside in the present moment ... The past is over and done with, and the future is not yet formed ... Attend, then, to the present— its sounds, its tastes and smells ... Enjoy the moment, and just Be ... Be the Silence ... Be the Wisdom ... Be the Joy ... Be the Love ... And as you do, the way will be made known ...

Yes, you are a citizen of the universe, a creation of God's own making ... Where you will be going, and what you will be doing will be beyond the farthest reaches of your imagination, for you are participating in the cosmic dance of life ... You can do this, for the inner reaches of your soul are boundless ...

So know now that you are Absolute Existence ... You are the Silence ... Rest in this knowledge, and know that you are the Unlimited Being ... and It is expressing Itself through you, as you, even now ...

So let this understanding settle within your conscious awareness ... even within your very heart ... Just rest in this knowledge ... and after you have done so, when you are ready, slowly open your eyes.

1. As you focused on the Silence all around you, were you able to see how your own awareness is silent, too?
2. Can you sense what "seed," what potential, is growing within you as your very own special way to serve?
3. Can you see how letting go of the past frees you to unfold more fully in the present moment?

Relaxing into Your Breath

In his book, *Full Catastrophe Living*, Dr. Jon Kabat-Zinn talks about learning to surf the waves of life. One of the tools that can help us do that is the breath. In fact, we could say the breath can act as our stabilizer as we work through the many changes that life presents.

The breath is our friend. It is always there for us, waiting for us to use it however we need to. Because our emotions—both positive and negative—have an immediate effect on our breathing, they may cause us to breathe faster, sigh, gasp, or even stop breathing momentarily. Becoming aware of our breath is an important way to gently steer our emotional responses into healthy patterns. As with all things, we begin by becoming aware.

Simply feeling the breath flowing in the nostrils is very centering, very calming. Focusing in this way can give you time to gain a clearer perspective on the events that are unfolding around you. If you can learn to shift your attention to the breath in the nostrils when anger is building, you can gain enough distance to choose an appropriate reaction or response.

Maintaining a flow of steady breathing is an important tool when we are confronted with anxiety, sadness, and depression. And when we are feeling stressed, if we pay attention to our breathing, we may sense how the tension in the body is restricting our breathing. When we notice these signals, deep breathing helps the body relax and the mind think more clearly.

When experiencing physical pain, it helps to bring your attention to the breath and deepen it. Use your breathing to join the pain rather than fighting with it. Try to bring your attention more and more to the breath and less and less to the pain. Focusing on the breath allows you to notice the pain but not engage with it. That little bit of separation can bring relief.

Dr. Deepak Chopra teaches a particularly effective tool to use when sudden emotional distress arises. When things happen suddenly, as they sometimes do, Dr. Chopra says to place your attention in your heart and breathe slowly and deeply. Emotions are energy surges. This technique helps calm the waves and quiet the waters of the mind.

When we relax into our breath, the breath flows easily, moving in and out of the lungs freely as it draws on a limitless supply. The following steps help develop breath awareness. These can be done sitting up or lying on your back.

1. Close your eyes. Using your breath to help you, relax your feet and legs, then your abdomen, your back, your arms, your hands, the sides of your rib cage. Allow your neck and head to relax deeply. Pay attention to the ears, the eyes, the cheek bones, the tongue, the chin. Feel how each inhalation and exhalation cleanses and nourishes you as you do this.

2. As you settle into keeping your attention on the breath, don't try to control it. Just let the breath be what it is. It will find its own balance and its own rhythm.

3. Once your breathing settles into a steady pattern, your body and your mind become quieter.

4. Without trying to control it, let your breath become deep and smooth, flowing without pause, as though your whole body is breathing.

5. You'll notice, too, how focusing on the breath anchors you in the present moment, so you aren't losing yourself in thoughts about the past or the future. If you do have a thought, just bring your attention gently back to the breath.

6. If you can, try watching your breath for ten to twenty minutes, or whatever length of time is comfortable for you.
7. Then just rest quietly for a moment before you open your eyes and continue on with your day.

Practicing breath awareness once or twice a day develops a sense of inner peace and stability and makes it easier to meet what each day brings. If this practice speaks to you, find a time when you can stop and relax into the breath consistently each and every day. When relaxing into the breath becomes part of the rhythm of your life, maximum benefits are sure to follow.

Bibliography

Reading played such an important part in my recovery. It gave me access to areas I had no other way to explore and gave me a sounding board that helped me find what rang true within me. The books I discovered broadened my perception and my sense of identity immeasurably.

While the list here isn't complete, it's a good sampling of what helped me. I've broken the list into categories to make it a little easier to digest. Some of these books may no longer be in print, but don't let that stop you. Oftentimes it's possible to find used copies, even at a greatly reduced price.

If something you see here strikes a chord within you, then by all means follow through on that impulse. That's what I did, and it made all the difference.

ALTERNATIVE THERAPIES

Beaulieu, John. *Music and Sound in the Healing Arts: An Energy Approach.* Barrytown, N.Y.: Station Hill Press, 1987.

Bradford, Michael. *The Healing Energy of Your Hands.* Freedom, Calif.: The Crossing Press, 1993.

Campbell, Don G. *The Roar of Silence.* Wheaton, Ill.: Theosophical Publishing House, 1989.

Cohen, Kenneth S. *The Way of Qigong*. New York: Ballantine Books, 1997.

DeMohan, Elias. *The Harmonics of Sound, Color & Vibration*. Marina del Rey, Calif.: DeVorss, 1994.

Eden, Donna. *Energy Medicine*. New York: Tarcher/Putnam, 1998.

Emoto, Masuru. *The Message of Water*. Tokyo: Hado Publishing, 2001.

Frawley, Dr. David. *Ayurveda and the Mind: The Healing of Consciousness*. Twin Lakes, Wisc.: Lotus Press, 1996.

- *The Yoga of Herbs*. Twin Lakes, Wisc.: Lotus Press, 1988.

Frawley, Dr. David and Ranade, Dr. Subhash. *Ayurveda: Nature's Medicine*. Twin Lakes, Wisc.: Lotus Press, 2001.

Gach, Michael Reed. *Acupressure's Potent Points*. New York: Bantam, 1990.

Goldman, Jonathan. *Healing Sounds: The Power of Harmonics*. Boston: Element Books, 1996.

- *Shifting Frequencies*. Sedona, Ariz.: Light Technology Publishing, 1998.

Hendricks, Gay. *Conscious Breathing*. New York: Bantam Books, 1995.

Keyes, Laurel Elizabeth. *Toning: The Creative Power of the Voice*. Marina del Rey, Calif.: DeVorss, 1997.

Leeds, Joshua. *Sonic Alchemy*. Sausalito, Calif.: Inner Song Press, 1999.

Liang, Master Shou-Yu. *Qigong Empowerment*. East Providence, R.I.: The Way of the Dragon, 1997.

Maman, Fabian. *The Role of Music in the 21st Century, Book 1*. Poland: Tama-Do Press, 1997.

Rick, Stephanie. *The Reflexology Workout*. New York: Crown Trade Paperback, 1986.

Tse, Michael. *Qigong for Health and Vitality*. New York: St. Martin's Griffin, 1995.

Worwood, Valerie Ann. *The Complete Book of Essential Oils & Aromatherapy*. New York: New World Library, 1991.

ANCIENT WISDOM TRADITIONS

Abhedenanda, Swami. *Journey into Kashmir and Tibet.* Calcutta: Ramakrishna Vedanta Math, 2001.

Aurobindo, Sri. *Bhagavad Gita and Its Message.* Twin Lakes, Wisc.: Lotus Press, 1995.

- *The Essential Aurobindo.* Great Barrington, Mass.: Lindisfarne Books, 2001.

- *The Hour of God.* Pondicherry, India: Sri Aurobindo Ashram, 1998.

- *The Integral Yoga.* Twin Lakes, Wisc.: Lotus Press, 2000.

- *The Life Divine.* Pondicherry, India: Sri Aurobindo Ashram Press, 2004.

- *The Synthesis of Yoga.* Twin Lakes, Wisc.: Lotus Light Publications, 1996.

- *The Upanishads.* Twin Lakes, Wisc.: Lotus Press, 2001.

Balsekar, Ramesh S. *A Duet of One, The Ashtavakra Dialogue.* Los Angeles: Advaita Press, 1989.

- *Consciousness Speaks.* Redondo Beach, Calif.: Advaita Press, 1992.

- *The Final Truth.* Redondo Beach, Calif.: Advaita Press, 1989.

Chimnoy, Sri. *The Silent Teaching.* Edinburg: Citadel Books, 1992.

Chopra, Dr. Deepak. *Buddha, A Story of Enlightenment.* San Francisco: Harper, 2007.

Easwaren, Eknath. *The Bhagavad Gita.* Tomales, Calif.: Nilgiri Press, 1985.

- *The Upanishads.* Tomales, Calif.: Nilgiri Press, 1987.

Feuerstein, Georg; Kak, Subhash; and Frawley, Dr. David. *In Search of the Cradle of Civilization.* Wheaton, Ill.: Quest Books, 2001.

Frawley, Dr. David. *Beyond the Mind.* Delhi: Sri Satguru Publications, 1984.

- *From the River of Heaven.* Salt Lake City: Passage Press, 1990.

- *Gods, Sages and Kings.* Delhi: Motilal Banarsidass Publishers, 1999.

- *Wisdom of the Ancient Seers, Mantras of the Rig Veda.* Salt Lake City: Passage Press, 1992.

- *Yoga & Ayurveda: Self-Healing and Self Realization.* Twin Lakes, Wisc.: Lotus Press, 1999.

Govindan, Marshall. *Kriya Yoga Sutras of Patanjali and the Siddhas.* Eastman, Quebec: Kriya Yoga Publications, 2000.

Grimes, John. *A Concise Dictionary of Indian Philosophy.* Albany: State University of New York Press, 1989.

Hawley, Jack. *The Bhagavad Gita: A Walkthrough for Westerners.* Novato, Calif.: New World Library, 2001.

Hesse, Hermann. *Siddhartha.* New York: Bantam Books, 1951.

Kriyananda, Goswami. *The Spiritual Science of Kriya Yoga.* Chicago: The Temple of Kriya Yoga, 1992.

Maharaj, Sri Nisargadatta. *Consciousness and the Absolute.* Durham, N.C.: Acorn Press, 1994.

- *I Am That.* Durham, N.C.: Acorn Press, 1973.

- *Prior to Consciousness.* Durham, N.C.: Acorn Press, 1997.

- *Seeds of Consciousness.* Durham, N.C.: Acorn Press, 1997.

- *The Experience of Nothingness.* San Diego: Blue Dove Press, 1996.

Maharshi, Sri Ramana. *Be As You Are.* London: Arkana, 1985.

- *Heart Is Thy Name, Oh Lord.* Tiruvannamalai, India: Sri Ramanasramam, 2004.

- *The Collected Works of Ramana Maharshi.* Tiruvannamalai, India: Sri Ramanasramam, 2004.

Nikhilananda, Swami. *Self-Knowledge.* New York: Ramakrishna Vivekananda Center, 1974.

Osborne, Arthur. *For Those with Little Dust: Pointers on the Teachings of Ramana Maharshi.* Inner Directions Publishing, 2001.

Osho. *Absolute TAO.* Pune, India: TAO Publishing, 2001.

- *The Book of Secrets.* St. Martin's Griffin, 1994.

Pandit, M.P. *Dictionary of Sri Aurobindo's Yoga.* Twin Lakes, Wisc.: Lotus Light Publications, 1992.

Prabhavananda, Swami. *How to Know God: The Yoga Aphorisms of Patanjali.* Hollywood, Calif.: Vedanta Press, 1981.

- *Shankara's Crest-Jewel of Discrimination.* Hollywood, Calif.: Vedanta Press, 1978.

- *The Sermon on the Mount According to Vedanta.* New York: New American Library, 1963.

Radha, Swami Sivananda. *Mantras: Words of Power.* Spokane: Timeless Books, 1996.

Rajagopalachari, G. *Mahabharata.* Bombay: Bharatiya Vidya Bhavan, 2006.

- *Ramayana.* Bombay: Bharatiya Vidya Bhavan, 2005.

Rama, Swami. *Living with the Himalayan Masters.* Honesdale, Penn.: Himalayan Institute Press, 1999.

- *Path of Fire and Light, Vol. 1.* Honesdale, Penn.: Himalayan Institute Press, 2004.

- *Samadhi, the Highest State of Wisdom, Yoga the Sacred Science.* Uttaranchal, India: Himalayan Institute Press, 2002.

Shearer, Alistair. *The Yoga Sutras of Patanjali.* New York: Random House, 2002.

Shraddhananda, Swami. *Seeing God Everywhere.* Hollywood, Calif.: Vedanta Press, 1996.

Spaulding, Baird T. *Life & Teaching of the Masters of the Far East, Vol. 1–5,* Marina del Rey, Calif.: DeVorss, 1964.

- *Vol. 6.* Marina del Rey, Calif.: DeVorss, 1996.

The Mother. *Rays of Light.* Pondicherry, India: Sri Aurobindo Ashram Press, 2004.

Thien-An, Thich. *Zen Philosophy, Zen Practice.* Berkeley, Calif.: Dharma Publishing, 1975.

Venkatesananda, Sri. *The Concise Yoga Vasistha.* Albany: State University of New York Press, 1984.

Vivekananda, Swami. *A Study of the Mundaka Upanishad.* Calcutta: Advaita Ashrama, 2000.

- *Karma Yoga.* Kolkota, India: Advaita Ashrama Publications, 2001.

- *Vedanta,* Voice of Freedom. St. Louis: Vedanta Society, 1986.

Yogananda, Paramahansa. *Autobiography of a Yogi.* Los Angeles: Self Realization Fellowship, 2001.

- *The Bhagavad Gita: God Talks with Arjuna, Vol. 1 & 2.* Los Angeles: Self Realization Fellowship, 1995.

Yukteswar, Swami Sri. *The Holy Science.* Los Angeles: Self Realization Fellowship, 1990.

DEATH AND DYING

Blackman, Sushila. *Graceful Exits: How Great Beings Die.* New York: Weatherhill, 1997.

Brinkley, Dannion. *Saved by the Light.* New York: Villard Books, 1994.

Chopra, Dr. Deepak. *Life After Death.* Harmony Books, 2006.

Collett, Merrill. *At Home with Dying, A Zen Hospice Approach.* Boston: Shambhala, 1999.

Eadie, Betty. *Embraced by the Light.* New York: Bantam Books, 1992.

Easwaran, Eknath. *Dialogue with Death.* Berkeley, Calif.: Nilgiri Press, 1992.

Morse, Melvin. *Parting Visions.* New York: Villard Books, 1994.

Rinpoche, Sogyal. *The Tibetan Book of Living and Dying.* San Francisco: Harper, 1994.

HATHA YOGA

Bennett, Bija. *Emotional Yoga.* New York: Fireside Books, 2002.

Chopra, Dr. Deepak. *The Seven Spiritual Laws of Yoga.* Hoboken, N.J.: John Wiley & Sons, 2004.

Coulter, H. David. *Anatomy of Hatha Yoga.* Honesdale, Penn.: Body & Breath, 2001.

Francina, Suza. *The New Yoga for People Over 50.* Deerfield Beach, Fla.: Health Communications, 1997.

Fraser, Tara. *The Easy Yoga Workbook.* London: Thorsons, 2003.

- *Yoga for Your Type.* Twin Lakes, Wisc.: Lotus Press, 2001.

Heriza, Nirmala. *Dr. Yoga.* New York: Tarcher/Penguin, 2004.

Iyengar, B.K.S. *Yoga: The Path to Holistic Health.* London: Dorling Kindersley, 2001.

Lasater, Judith. *30 Essential Yoga Poses.* Berkeley, Calif.: Rodmell Press, 2003.

Pinckney, Callan. *Callanetics Countdown.* New York: Random House, 1990.

HEALTH AND WELLNESS

Benson, Herbert. *Timeless Healing.* New York: Scribner, 1996.

Borysenko, Joan. *Minding the Body, Mending the Mind.* New York: Bantam Books, 1987.

Chopra, Dr. Deepak. *Ageless Body, Timeless Mind.* New York: Harmony Books, 1993.

- *Boundless Energy.* New York: Harmony Books, 1995.

- *Creating Health.* Boston: Houghton Mifflin, 1987.

- *Grow Younger, Live Longer.* New York: Harmony Books, 2001.

- *Healing the Heart.* New York: Harmony Books, 1998.

- *Journey Into Healing.* New York: Harmony Books, 1994.

- *Perfect Health.* New York: Harmony Books, 1991.

- *Quantum Healing.* New York: Bantam New Age Books, 1989.

- *Reinventing the Body, Resurrecting the Soul.* Harmony Books, 2009.

- *Unconditional Life.* New York: Bantam Books, 1991.

Cousins, Norman. *Anatomy of an Illness.* New York: Norton, 1979.

Myss, Carolyn. *Anatomy of the Spirit.* New York: Harmony Books, 1996.

- *Why People Don't Heal & How They Can.* New York: Harmony Books, 1997.

Nelson, Miriam. *Strong Women, Strong Bones.* New York: G.P. Putnam's Sons, 2000.

Pert, Candace. *Molecules of Emotion.* New York: Simon & Schuster Trade, 1997.

Siegel, Bernie. *How to Live Between Office Visits.* New York: HarperCollins, 1993.

- *Love, Medicine & Miracles.* New York: Harper & Row, 1986.

- *Peace, Love & Healing.* New York: Harper & Row, 1989.

- *Prescriptions for Living.* New York: HarperCollins, 1998.

Simon, Dr. David. *Free to Love, Free to Heal.* Chopra Center Press, 2009.

- *Return to Wholeness.* New York: John Wiley & Sons, 1999.

- *Vital Energy.* New York: John Wiley & Sons, 2000.

- *The Wisdom of Healing*. New York: Harmony Books, 1997.

Topf, Linda Noble. *You Are Not Your Illness*. New York: Simon & Schuster Trade Books, 1995.

Weil, Andrew. *Eat Well for Optimum Health*. New York: Alfred A. Knopf, 2000.

- *Health and Healing*. New York: Houghton Mifflin, 1983.

- *Natural Health, Natural Medicine*. Boston: Houghton Mifflin, 1995.

- *Spontaneous Healing*. New York: Alfred A. Knopf, 1995.

INSPIRATIONAL READING

Ambrose, Stephen E. *Undaunted Courage*. New York: Simon & Schuster, 1996.

Angland, Joan Walsh. *The Circle of the Spirit*. New York: Random House, 1983.

Bach, Marcus. *Illusions*. New York: Delacorte Press, 1977.

- *Jonathan Livingston Seagull*. New York: Macmillan, 1970.

Bentov, Itzhak. *Stalking the Wild Pendulum*. Rochester, Vt.: Destiny Books, 1988.

Braden, Gregg. *The Isaiah Effect*. New York: Harmony Books, 2000.

- *Walking Between the Worlds*. Bellevue, Wash.: Radio Bookstore Press, 1997.

Breathnach, Sarah Ban. *Simple Abundance*. New York: Warner Books, 1995.

Cameron, Julia. *The Artist's Way*. New York: G.P.Putnam's Sons, 1992.

Chopra, Dr. Deepak. *Creating Affluence*. San Rafael, Calif.: Amber-Allen, 1998.

- *Daughters of Joy*. New York: New American Library, 2002.

- *Everyday Immortality*. New York: Harmony Books, 1995.

- *How to Know God*. New York: Harmony Books, 2000.

- *Power, Freedom and Grace*. San Rafael: Amber-Allen, 2006.

- *Return of the Rishi*. Boston: Houghton Mifflin, 1988.

- *The Book of Secrets*. New York: Harmony House, 2004.

- *The Path to Love*. New York: Three Rivers Press, 1997.

- *The Return of Merlin*. New York: Harmony Books, 1995.

- *The Seven Spiritual Laws for Parents*. New York: Crown, 1997.

- *The Seven Spiritual Laws of Success*. San Rafael, Calif.: Amber-Allen, 1994.

- *The Spontaneous Fulfillment of Desire*. New York: Three Rivers Press, 2003.

- *The Way of the Wizard*. New York: Harmony Books, 1995.

Chopra, Gautama. *Child of the Dawn*. San Rafael, Calif.: Amber-Allen, 1996.

Dass, Ram. *Journey of Awakening*. New York: Bantam, 1978.

Easwaran, Eknath. *Gandhi The Man: The Story of His Transformation*. Tomales, Calif.: Nilgiri Press, 1997.

Feiler, Bruce. *Walking the Bible*. New York: William Morrow, 2001.

Ford, Debbie. *The Dark Side of the Light Chasers*. New York: Putnam Publishing Group, 1998.

Fox, Emmet. *Power Through Constructive Thinking*. San Gabriel, Calif.: Harper & Brothers, 1940.

- *The Sermon on the Mount*. New York: Harper & Brothers, 1938.

Fox, John. *Finding What You Didn't Lose*. New York: Jeremy P. Tarcher, 1995.

- *Poetic Medicine*. New York: Jeremy P. Tarcher, 1997.

Ganesan, V. *Drops from the Ocean*. Tiruvannamalai, India: Ananda Ramana, 2005.

Gibran, Kahlil. *The Prophet*. New York: Alfred A. Knopf, 2002.

Goswami, Amit. *The Self-Aware Universe*. New York: Jeremy P. Tarcher, 1995.

Grey, Alex. *Sacred Mirrors: The Visionary Art of Alex Grey*. Rochester, Vt.: Inner Traditions International, 1990.

Harvey, Andrew. *Hidden Journey*. New York: Penguin, 1992.

Hawkins, Dr. David. *Power vs Force*. Sedona, Ariz.: Veritas, 1995. [This is the first in a series. All are excellent.]

Johnson, Robert A. *Balancing Heaven and Earth*. San Francisco: Harper, 1998.

Kabat-Zinn, Dr. Jon. *Full Catastrophe Living*. New York: Delta Books, 1990.

- *Wherever You Go There You Are*. New York: Hyperion Books, 1994.

Keller, Helen. *Light in My Darkness*. West Chester, Penn.: Chrysalis Books, 1994.

Kharitidi, Olga. *Entering the Circle*. San Francisco: Harper, 1996.

Killinger, John. *Bread for the Wilderness, Wine for the Journey*. Nashville, Tenn.: Word Books, 1976.

Krishnamurti, J. and Bohm, Dr. David. *The Ending of Time*. San Francisco: HarperCollins, 1985.

Lama, The Dalai. *An Open Heart*. Boston: Time Warner, 2001.

- *The Art of Happiness*. New York: Riverhead Books, 1998.

L'Engle, Madelaine. *The Irrational Season*. New York: Farrar, Strauss & Giroux, 1987.

Leonard, George and Murphy, Michael. *The Life You Are Given*. New York: Putnam, 1995.

Levoy, Gregg. *Callings, Finding and Following an Authentic Life*. New York: Three Rivers Press, 1997.

Mitchell, Dr. Edgar. *The Way of the Explorer*. New York: G.P. Putnam's Sons, 1996.

Moore, Thomas. *The Care and Feeding of the Soul*. New York: HarperCollins, 1992.

Morehouse, Dr. David. *Psychic Warrior*. New York: St. Martin's Press, 1996.

Mountain Dreamer, Oriah. *The Invitation*. San Francisco: Harper, 1999.

Naparstek, Belleruth. *Your Sixth Sense*. San Francisco: Harper, 1997.

Neal, Viola Petitt. *Through the Curtain*. Marina del Rey, Calif.: DeVorss, 1983.

Norris, Kathleen. *The Cloister Walk*. New York: Riverhead Books, 1996.

Nouwen, Henri. *The Wounded Healer*. Garden City, N.Y.: Image Books, 1979.

O'Donohue, John. *Anam Cara, A Book of Celtic Wisdom*. New York: Cliff Street Books, 1997.

-Eternal Echoes, *Celtic Reflections on Our Yearning to Belong*. New York: Cliff Street Books, 2000.

O'Leary, Brian. *Exploring Inner and Outer Space*. Berkeley, Calif.: North Atlantic Books, 1989.

Orloff, Judith. *Second Sight*. New York: Warner Books, 1996.

Osborne, Arthur. *For Those with Little Dust*. Carlsbad, Calif.: Inner Directions Publishing, 2001.

Peirce, Penney. *The Intuitive Way*. New York: MJF Books, 1995.

Powell, Robert. *Beyond Religion*. San Diego: Blue Dove Press, 2001.

Rama, Swami. *The Art of Joyful Living*. Honesdale, Penn. Himalayan Institute, 2003.

Ramtha. *Ramtha*. Bellevue, Wash.: Sovereignty, 1986.

Redfield, James. *The Celestine Prophecy*. New York: Warner Books, 1993.

Roberts, Jane. *Seth Speaks*. Englewood Cliffs, N.J.: Prentice-Hall, 1972.

- *The Nature of Personal Reality*. New York: Bantam Books, 1988.

Sagan, Carl. *Pale Blue Dot*. New York: Random House, 1994.

St. James, Elaine. *Inner Simplicity*. New York: Hyperion Books, 1995.

- *Living the Simple Life*. New York: Hyperion Books, 1996.

- *Simplify Your Life*. New York: Hyperion Books, 1994.

Simon, Dr. David. *The Ten Commitments*. Deerfield Beach, Fla.: Health Communications, 2006.

Sinetar, Martha. *Holy Work*. New York: Crossroad Publishing, 1998.

- *To Build the Life You Want, Create the Work You Love*. New York: St. Martin's Press, 1995.

Skog, Susan. *Embracing Our Essence*. Deerfield Beach, Fla.: Health Communications, 1995.

Smoke, Jim. *Turning Points*. Eugene, Ore.: Harvest House, 1985.

Steiner, Rudolf. *How to Know Higher Worlds*. Hudson, N.Y.: Anthroposophic Press. 1994.

Taber, Gladys. *Another Path*. Philadelphia: Lippincott, 1963.

- *Stillmeadow Sampler*. Philadelphia: Lippincott, 1959.

Thornton, James. *A Field Guide to the Soul*. New York: Bell Tower, 1999.

Todeschi, Kevin. *Edgar Cayce on the Akashic Records*. Virginia Beach, Va.: A.R.E. Press, 1998.

Tolle, Eckhart. *The Power of Now*. Novato, Calif.: New World Library, 1999.

Tompkins, Peter. *The Secret Life of Nature*. San Francisco: Harper, 1997.

Twitchell, Paul. *Stranger by the River*. Menlo Park, Calif.: IWP Publishing, 1983.

- *The Flute of God*. Menlo Park, Calif.: IWP Publishing, 1982.

Twyman, James F. *Emissary of Light, A Vision of Peace*. New York: Warner Books, 1997.

Vanauken, Sheldon. *A Severe Mercy*. London: Hodder & Stoughton, 1977.

Walsch, Neale Donald. *Conversations with God, Book 1*. New York: G.P. Putnam's Sons, 1996.

- *Book 2*. Charlottesville, Va.: Hampton Roads, 1997.

- *Book 3*. Charlottesville, Va.: Hampton Roads, 1998.

Williamson, Marianne. *A Return to Love*. New York: Harper Perennial, 1992.

Wolf, Fred Alan. *The Spiritual Universe*. Portsmouth, N.H.: Moment Point Press, 1999.

Yogananda, Paramahansa. *The Second Coming of Christ, Vol. 1 & 2*. Los Angeles: SRF, 2004.

- *Wine of the Mystic, The Rubaiyat of Omar Khayyam, A Spiritual Interpretation*. Los Angeles: SRF, 1996.

Zukav, Gary. *The Seat of the Soul*. New York: Fireside Books, 1990.

PRAYER AND MEDITATION

Cowman, Mrs. Charles E. *Streams in the Desert*. Grand Rapids, Mich.: Zondervan, 1965.

DaPassano, Andrew. *Inner Silence*. San Francisco: Perennial Library, 1987.

deMello, Anthony. *Sadhana: A Way to God*. Garden City, N.Y.: Image Books, 1984.

Fittipaldi, Silvio E. *How to Pray Always*. Liguori, Mo.: Liguori Publications, 1985.

Goleman, Daniel. *The Meditative Mind*. New York: Putnam, 1988.

Frawley, Dr. David. *Vedantic Meditation: Lighting the Flame of Awareness*. Berkeley, Calif.: North Atlantic Books, 2000.

Keating, Abbot Thomas; Pennington, Basil; and Clarke, Thomas. *Finding Grace at the Center.* Still River, Mass.: St. Bede Publications, 1978.

Khalsa, Dharma Singh. *Meditation as Medicine.* New York: Pocket Books, 2001.

Klein, Jean. *I AM.* Salisbury, U.K.: Non-Duality Press, 1989.

Oates, Wayne E. *Nurturing Silence in a Noisy Heart.* Minneapolis: Augsburg, 1996.

Osho. *Meditation: The First and Last Freedom.* New York: St. Martin's Griffin, 1996.

- *The Book of Secrets.* New York: St. Martin's Griffin, 1974.

Pennington, M. Basil. *Centered Living.* New York: Doubleday, 1988.

Rama, Swami. *Meditation and Its Practice.* Honesdale, Penn.: Himalayan Institute Press, 1998.

Acknowledgments

As I look back over how this story was written, it occurs to me that this is not just my story. This is the story of all those whose lives were woven together to create this story, so I want to thank you all, for I would not be where I am today had you not been there helping make this story unfold.

There are far too many to mention. Everyone who has touched my life has played a part in this in some way, but I certainly would like to start by mentioning Mother, Daddy, Neal, and our children. The memories of how we did this together are precious beyond words.

I will never forget Dr. Deepak Chopra, Dr. David Simon, Jonathan Goldman, and Roger Gabriel, how they came into my life and helped shape it into something new and wonderful. Because of their teachings, because of their examples, I was able to find the part of me I'd always been looking for but had never quite been able to access. In learning how to see myself with clearer, truer vision, I also began to see others more truly as well, and so it was that the shadows began slipping away, allowing the Light—that beautiful Light—that amazing Presence—to become a conscious part of my life.

Through it all, children, friends, family near and far have played a part in this. That's why this is our story, not just my story, and in some way it must be your story, too, or you would not be reading this.

My deepest thanks to Hummer and Roz for all the love and all the joy—and the story—we have shared. You have filled my heart to overflowing.

My thanks as well to Barb Doyen, who hung in there with me and encouraged me from the time she first learned of my desire to share my journey with others. Her willingness to steer me through the early stages of this book was invaluable, and I am fortunate to have her for my friend.

Kudos, too, to Lisa Pelto, my faithful publisher and friend; to Sandra Wendel for her unselfish counsel; and Tara Knapp, whose sharp eye and ear helped bring the early stages of this story into focus.

And last, but certainly not least, I would like to thank Dr. David Morehouse, not only for generously offering to write the Foreword for this book, but also for expanding my horizons in ways I find impossible to describe.

To you all, I am grateful—from the bottom of my heart.

About the Author

Donna Miesbach has been on a spiritual path all her life. That path led her to extensive study with some of today's premier teachers of spirituality.

Donna has studied with Dr. Deepak Chopra for over fifteen years and is one of the Chopra Center's certified meditation and yoga instructors. She has studied extensively with Dr. David Morehouse and has achieved the level of Quantum Explorer in Remote Viewing. She has also completed the advanced level of intensive training in Sound Healing with Jonathan Goldman and is a member of the Sound Healers Association. She has studied with Roger Gabriel both in the United States and in India.

Other books by Donna Miesbach include *Trails of Stardust, Poems of Inspiration & Insight; Coaching for a Bigger Win: A Playbook for Coaches* with Greg "Coach Roz" Roeszler; and *Wise Women Speak: 20 Ways to Turn Stumbling Blocks into Stepping Stones* (guest author).

Donna has been a contributor to Unity Magazine and Daily Word since 1983. She was named "Inspirational Poet of the Year" by *The Poet Magazine* in 1985.

In addition to her writing and teaching, Donna is the Administrative Assistant to Greg Roeszler, the Executive Director of the California-based Playmakers Mentoring Foundation. Together they co-founded the Omaha chapter.

More information about Donna's writing and teaching is available on her website at www.DonnaMiesbach.com. To receive her "Thought for the Day," go to www.PonderPearls.com/Donna and click on "Register."

Donna lives and teaches in Omaha, Nebraska, and is blessed with a blended family of six children, thirteen grandchildren, and eight great grandchildren.

Printed in Great Britain
by Amazon